POESIE DES ABSURDEN

POETRY OF THE INCREDIBLE

Jonas C. Haefeli

BENTELI

Angeregt durch meinen Vater, welcher neben seiner wissenschaftlichen Tätigkeit ein begnadeter Maler und Zeichner war, malte ich als Kind sehr viel. Nicht wie mein Vater Berge und Landschaften, sondern üppig wuchernde, von Henri Rousseau inspirierte Urwälder mit wilden Tieren, Papageien, Elefanten, Giraffen und Krokodilen, wie sie auch in meinen späteren Bildern immer wieder anzutreffen sind, wenn auch in einem etwas anderen Umfeld. Andere Interessen hatte ich kaum, nicht einmal für die Musik, welche später mein Leben doch wesentlich dominieren sollte. Die Malerei war mein Ein und Alles. Ich war etwa zwölf Jahre alt, als ich zum ersten Mal ein Bild von Salvador Dalí sah, diese sich auflösende, schwerelose und zerfließende Realität, gemalt in einer absolut perfekten, altmeisterlichen Technik fand ich so faszinierend, dass ich umgehend beschloss, Kunstmaler zu werden. Also richtete ich mir im Heizungskeller ein »Atelier« ein und malte großformatige »Dalí-Bilder«, natürlich in Öl, wie es sich für einen »richtigen« Künstler gehörte. Einige Zeit später entdeckte ich dann den Surrealisten René Magritte. Das war, etwas pathetisch ausgedrückt, mein malerischer Urknall, welcher bis heute nachhallt. Magritte war weniger spektakulär, sondern subtiler, poetischer und geheimnisvoller. Nach und nach kamen immer mehr auch Einflüsse der anderen Surrealisten, sowie Maler des Phantastischen Realismus und Maler der jüngeren Generation dazu, bis ich zu meinem Stil fand.

Letztlich wurde ich dann doch nicht Maler, sondern Film- und Theaterkomponist und Musiker. Aber das ist eine andere Geschichte.

Inspired by my father, who was a gifted painter and draftsman in addition to his scientific activities, I painted a lot as a child. Not like my father mountains and landscapes, but lush sprawling jungles inspired by Henri Rousseau with wild animals, parrots, elephants, giraffes and crocodiles, as they are also in my later paintings again and again, even if in a somewhat different environment. I had hardly any other interests, not even for music, which was later to dominate my life considerably. Painting was my one and everything. I was about twelve years old when I first saw a painting by Salvador Dalí, this dissolving, weightless and flowing reality, painted in an absolutely perfect, old-masterly technique, I found so fascinating that I immediately decided to become a painter. So I set up a "studio" in the heating celler and painted large-format "Dalí pictures", of course in oil, as it belonged to a "real" artist. Some time later I discovered the surrealist René Magritte. That was, somewhat pathetically expressed, my painterly big bang, which reverberates to this day. Magritte was less spectacular, but more subtle, poetic and mysterious. Little by little more and more influences of the other Surrealists, as well as painters of Fantastic Realism and painters of the younger generation until I found my style.

In the end, I didn't become a painter, but a film and theater composer and a musician. But that's another story.

Jonas C.

Die Wahrscheinlichkeit, dass etwas sehr Unwahrscheinliches eintrifft, ist größer als man denkt

The probability of something very improbable happening is greater than you think

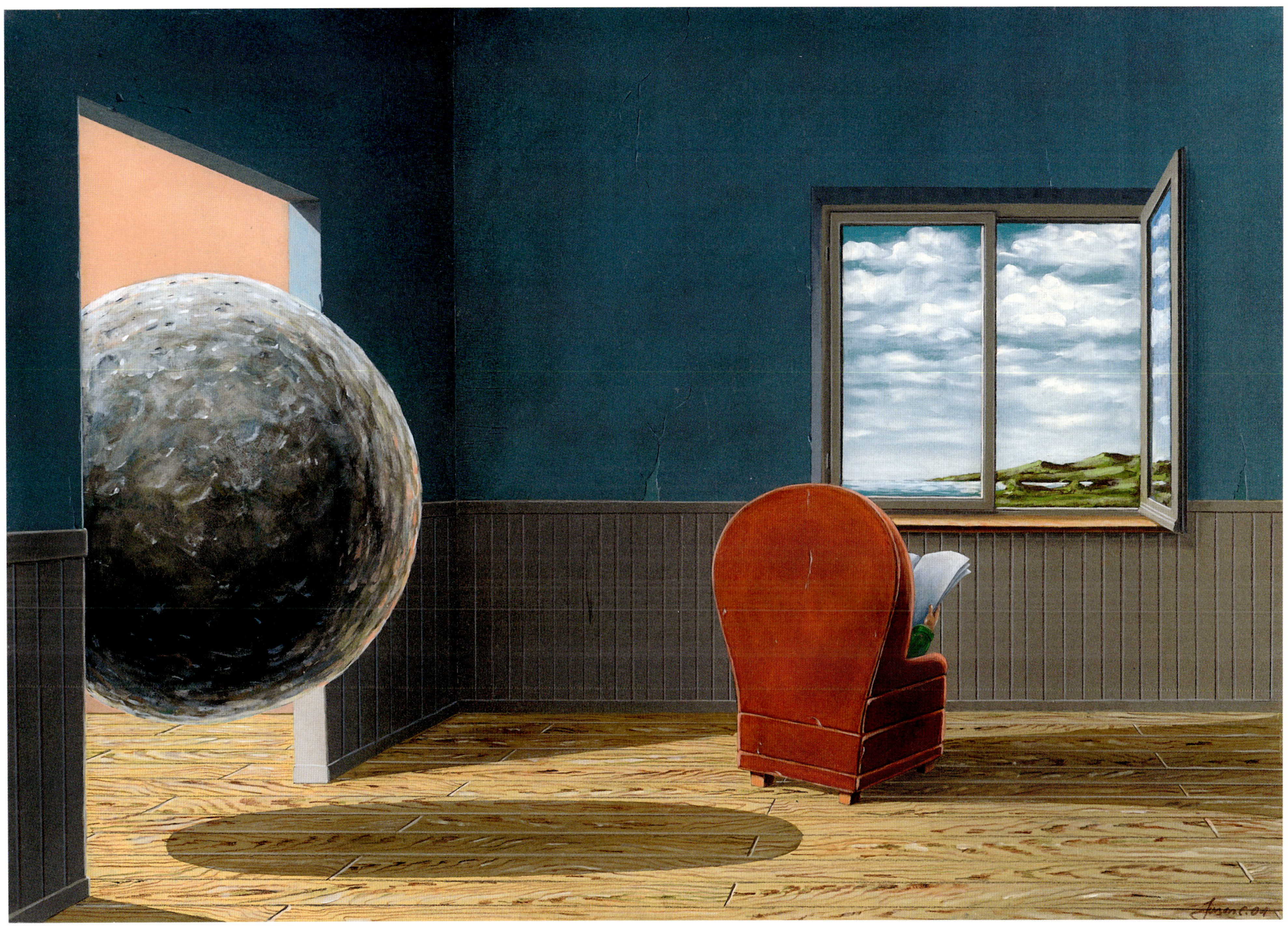

<u>2007</u>

Büro für außergewöhnliche Angelegenheiten und besonders schwere Fälle	Office for Exceptional Matters and Particularly Serious Cases

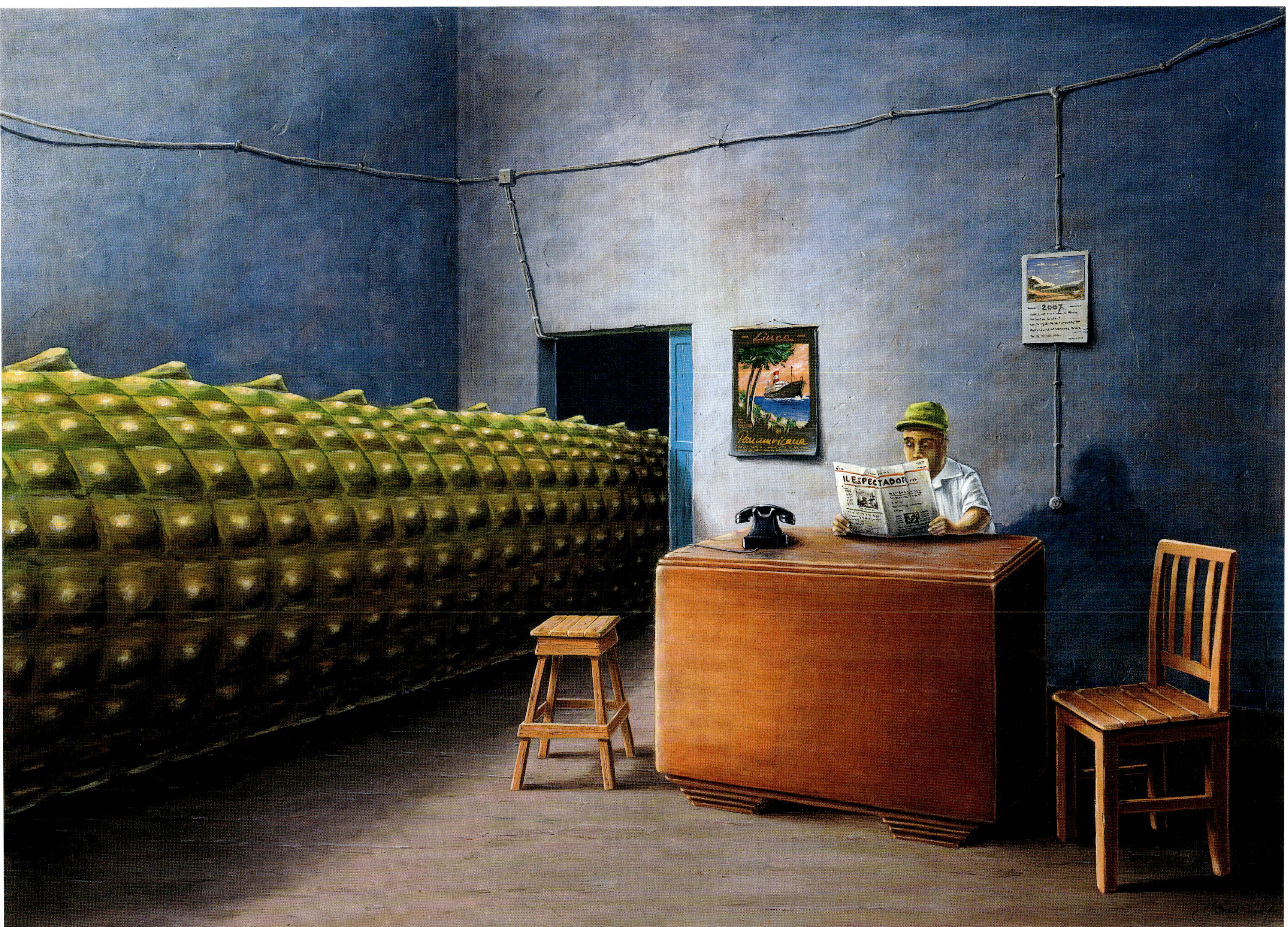
Linea
Panamericana
IL ESPECTADOR
2007

Dampfbetriebene Blechzeppeline sind konventionellen Zeppelinen in Bezug auf Stabilität, Sicherheit und Wirtschaftlichkeit in jeder Hinsicht weit überlegen. (Science-Magazine, 15.12.1908).

Steam-powered tin zeppelins are vastly superior to conventional zeppelins in terms of stability, safety and economy in every respect. (Science Magazine, 12.15.1908).

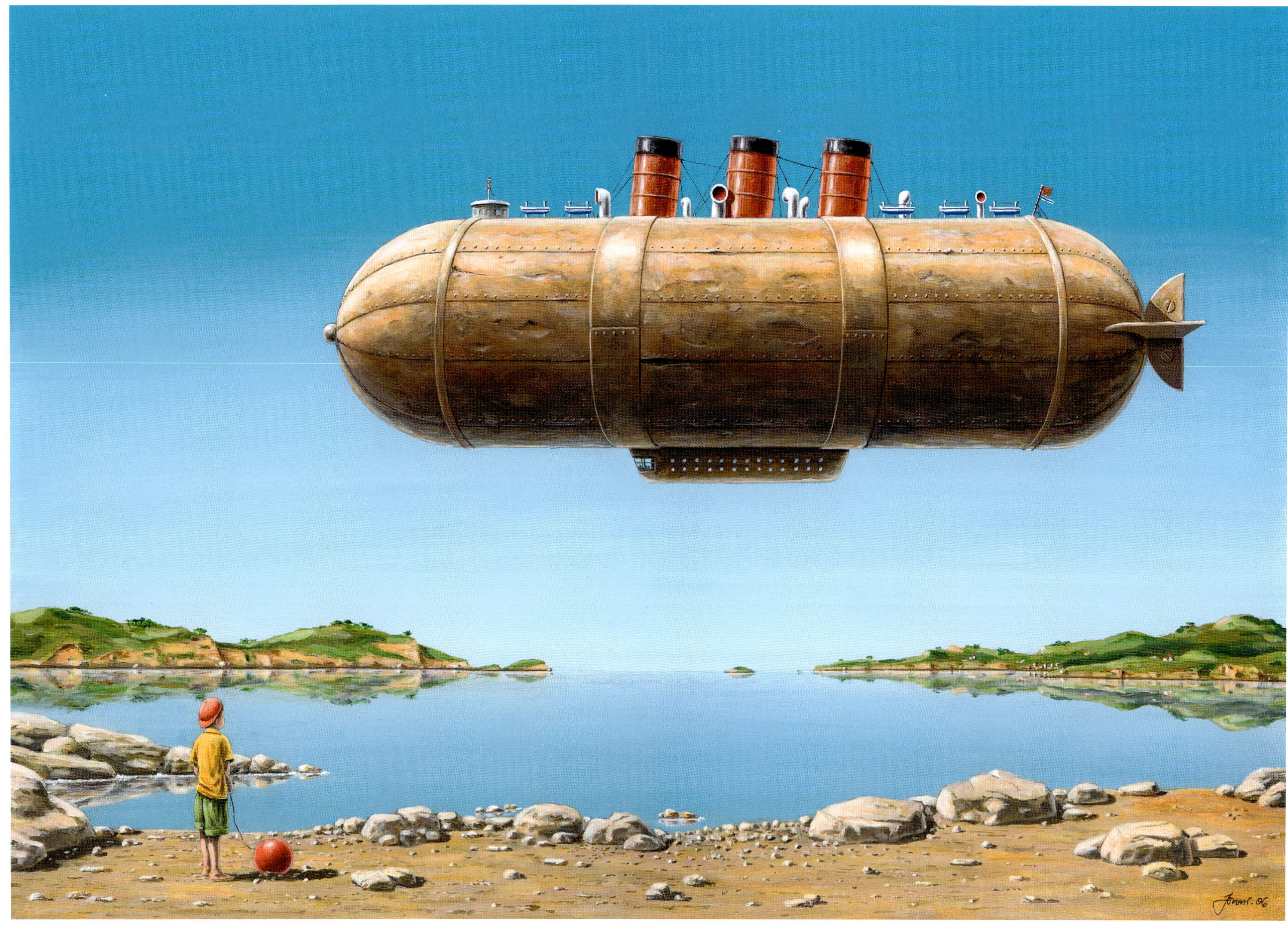

Am 23. April 1911 fanden in den frühen Morgenstunden spielende Kinder diese prächtige, äußerst seltene, große Augenmuschel (concha oculis magnus), welche von den Einheimischen kurzerhand liebevoll »la piccola Ernestina« getauft wurde. Nach ein paar Tagen verschwand sie mitten in der Nacht, von den Dorfbewohnern völlig unbemerkt, genau so geheimnisvoll, wie sie ein paar Tage zuvor aufgetaucht war wieder im Meer und wurde nie mehr gesehen.
Der Tag ihres Erscheinens wird seither mit einem großen Volksfest gefeiert und dabei das mittlerweile weltberühmte größte Muschelessen der Welt veranstaltet, welches jedes Jahr tausende von Touristen in das kleine Fischerdörfchen Porto Generoso lockt.
(Sagra della piccola Ernestina).

On April 23, 1911, in the early morning hours, playing children found this magnificent, extremely rare large eye shell (concha oculis magnus), which was affectionately christened "la piccola Ernestina" by the locals. After a few days she disappeared in the middle of the night, completely unnoticed by the villagers, back into the sea, just as mysteriously as she had appeared a few days before and was never seen again.
The day of her appearance is celebrated since then with a large folk festival and thereby the now world-famous largest mussel dinner in the world, which brings thousands of tourists every year to the small fishing village of Porto Generoso. (Sagra della piccola Ernestina).

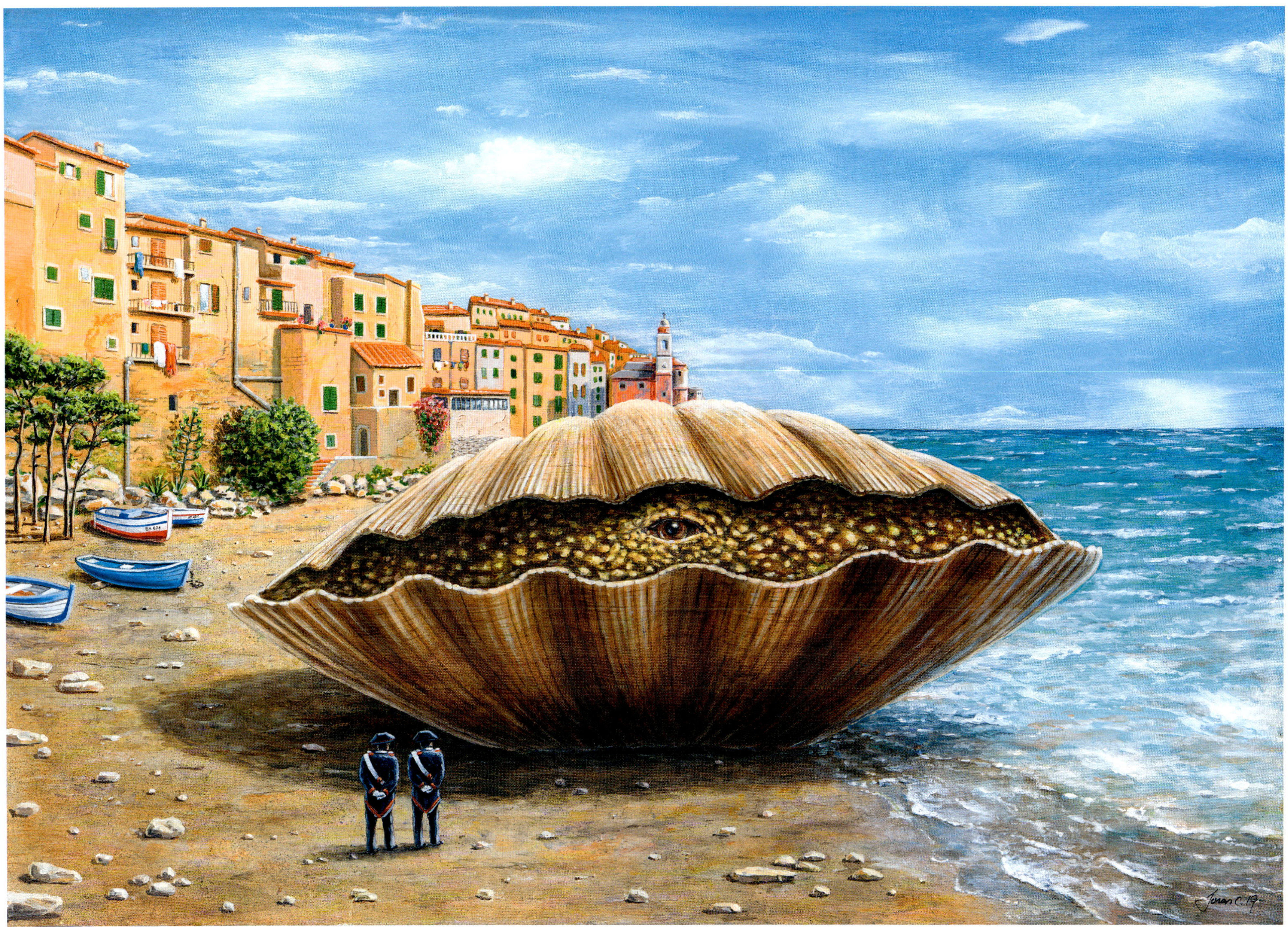

Die Fabel vom Walfisch
und der unsichtbaren Maus

The fable of the whale
and the invisible mouse

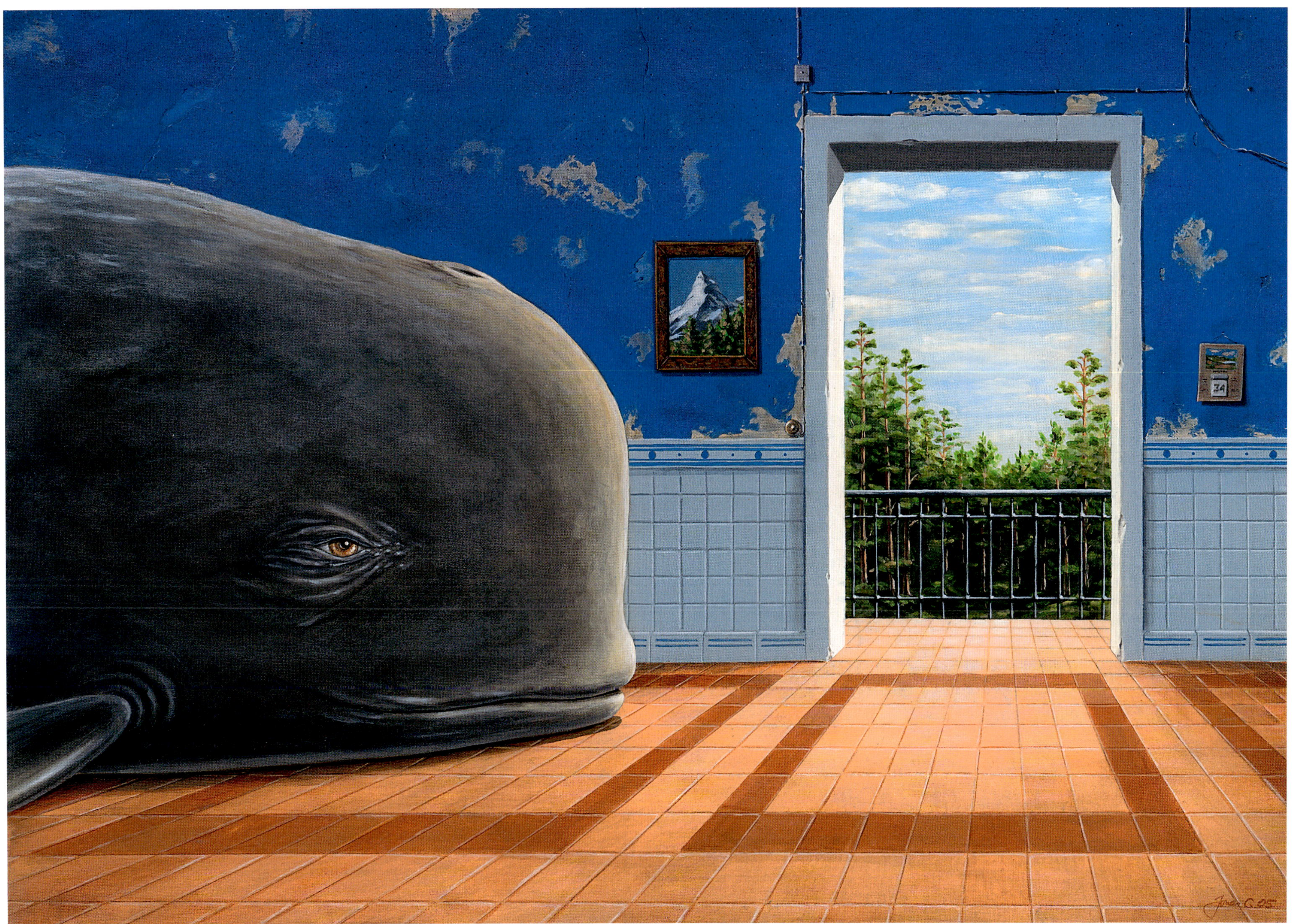

Die Einsamkeit des Joseph Carey Merrick, des wohl berühmtesten Elefantenmenschen aller Zeiten

The loneliness of Joseph Carey Merrick, probably the most famous elephant man of all times

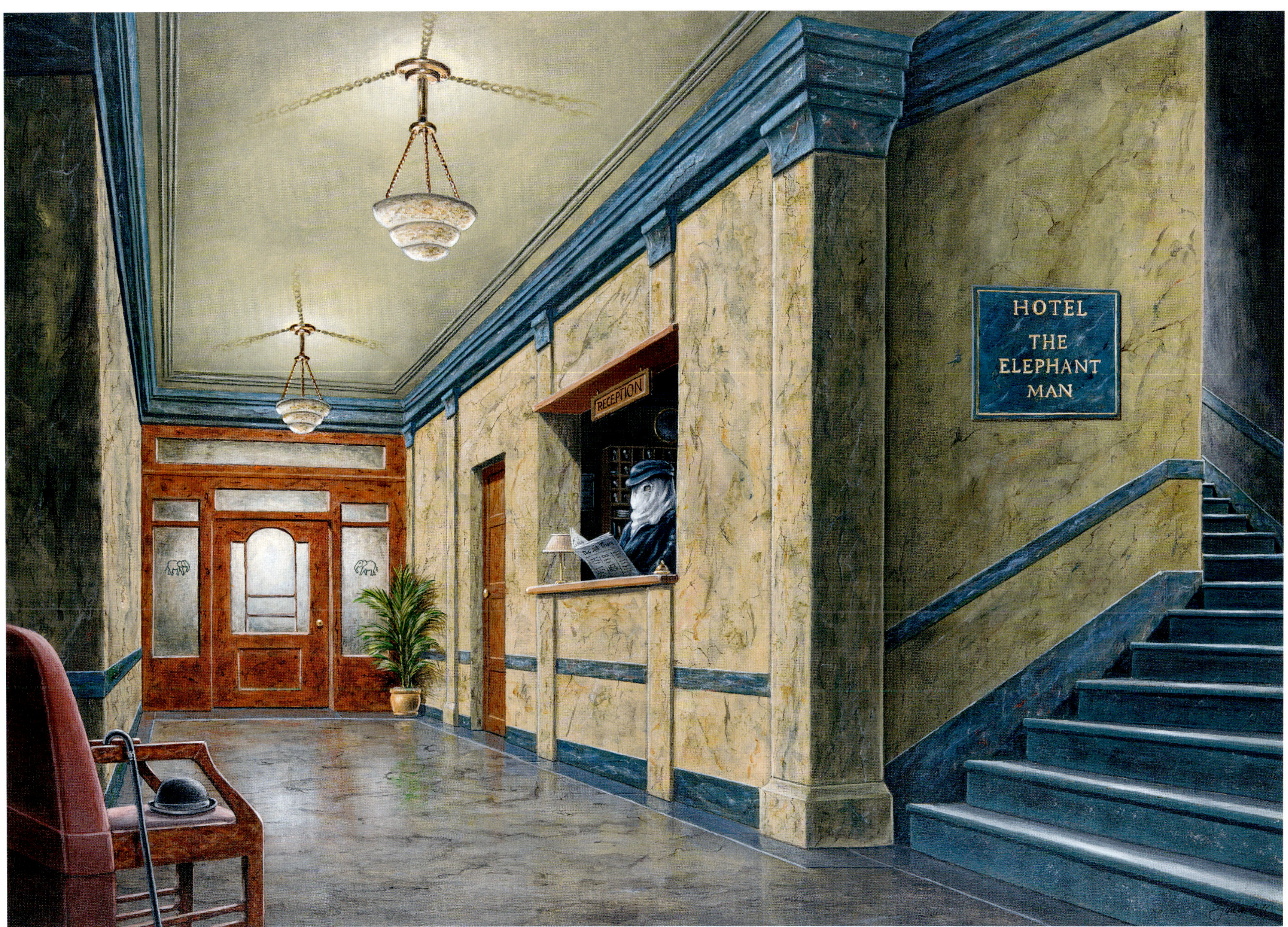
HOTEL
THE
ELEPHANT
MAN
RECEPTION

Eine etwas eigenartige, aber unvergessliche
»polonaise animale«

A somewhat peculiar but unforgettable
"polonaise animale"

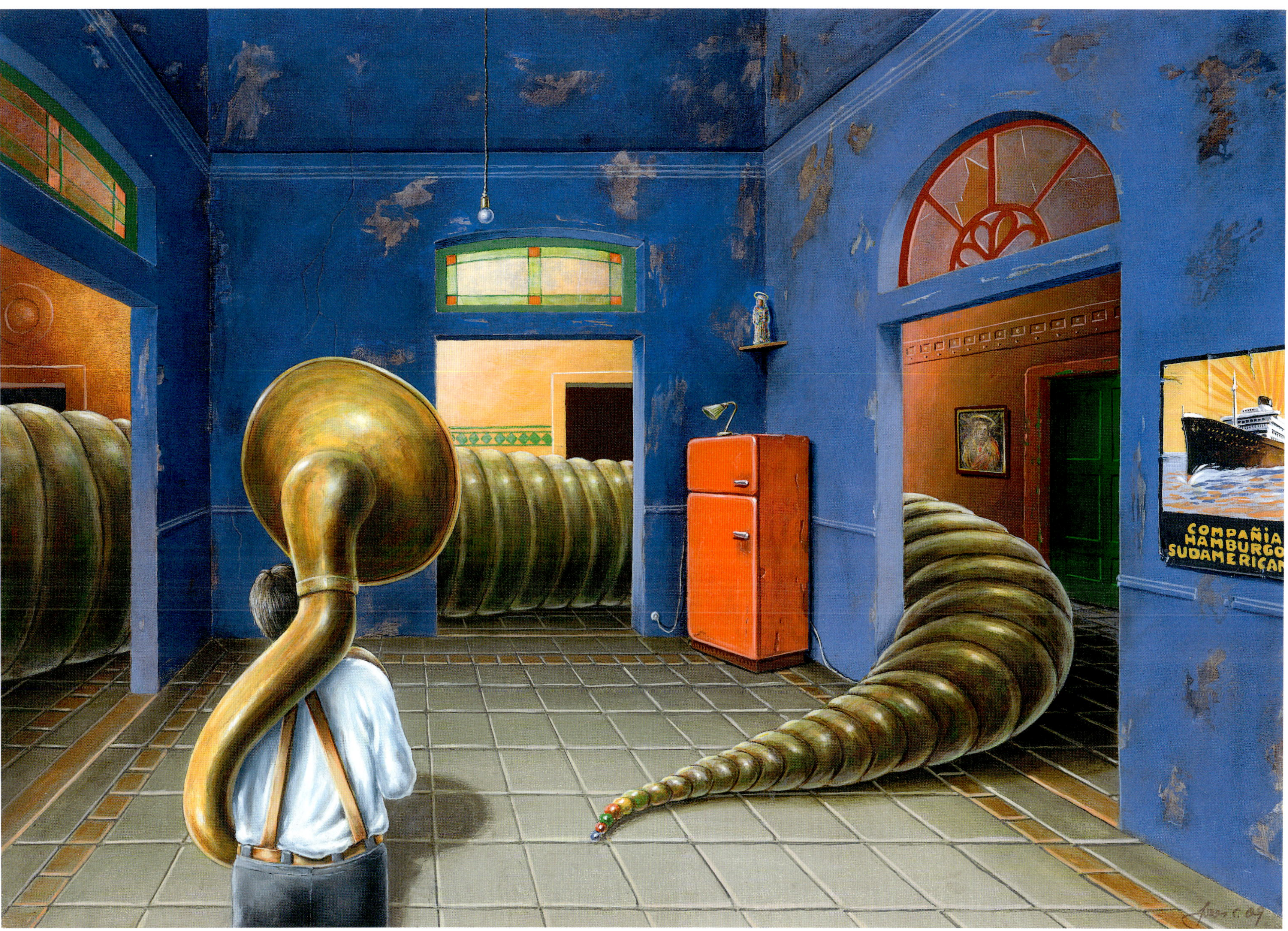

COMPAÑIA
HAMBURGO
SUDAMERICAN

Lars-Rüdiger, selbst ernannter Wolkenflüsterer, war überzeugt, dass er mit seinem selbstgebauten Gigafon mit den Wolken reden und sie beeinflussen könne. Das war natürlich kompletter Unsinn. Niemand glaubte ihm. Auch seine Freunde nahmen ihn nicht ernst, schätzten aber seine liebenswerte, wenn auch etwas schrullige Art und die Dorfbewohner waren heimlich doch auch etwas stolz auf ihn, da er, und damit auch das ganze Dorf, zu einer gewissen Berühmtheit gelangten.
Als er an einem wunderschönen wolkenlosen Sommertag im biblischen Alter von 102 Jahren starb, geschah allerdings etwas sehr, sehr Merkwürdiges:
Aus allen Himmelsrichtungen zogen – sprichwörtlich aus heiterem Himmel – über der Bucht Wolken auf und es begann ganz, ganz leise zu regnen und, wie Augenzeugen übereinstimmend berichteten, die Regentropfen waren leicht salzig, wie Tränen.

Lars-Rüdiger, self-proclaimed cloud whisperer, was convinced that he could talk to the clouds and influence them with his self-made gigaphone. This was, of course, complete nonsense. No one believed him, not even his friends took him seriously, but they appreciated his amiable, if somewhat quirky manner, and the villagers were secretly somewhat proud of him, since he, and with him the whole village, had achieved a certain fame. But when he died on a beautiful, cloudless summer day at the biblical age of 102 years, something very, very strange happened:
from all directions – literally out of the blue – clouds rose over the bay, and it began to rain very, very quietly – and, as eyewitnesses unanimously reported, the raindrops were slightly salty, like tears.

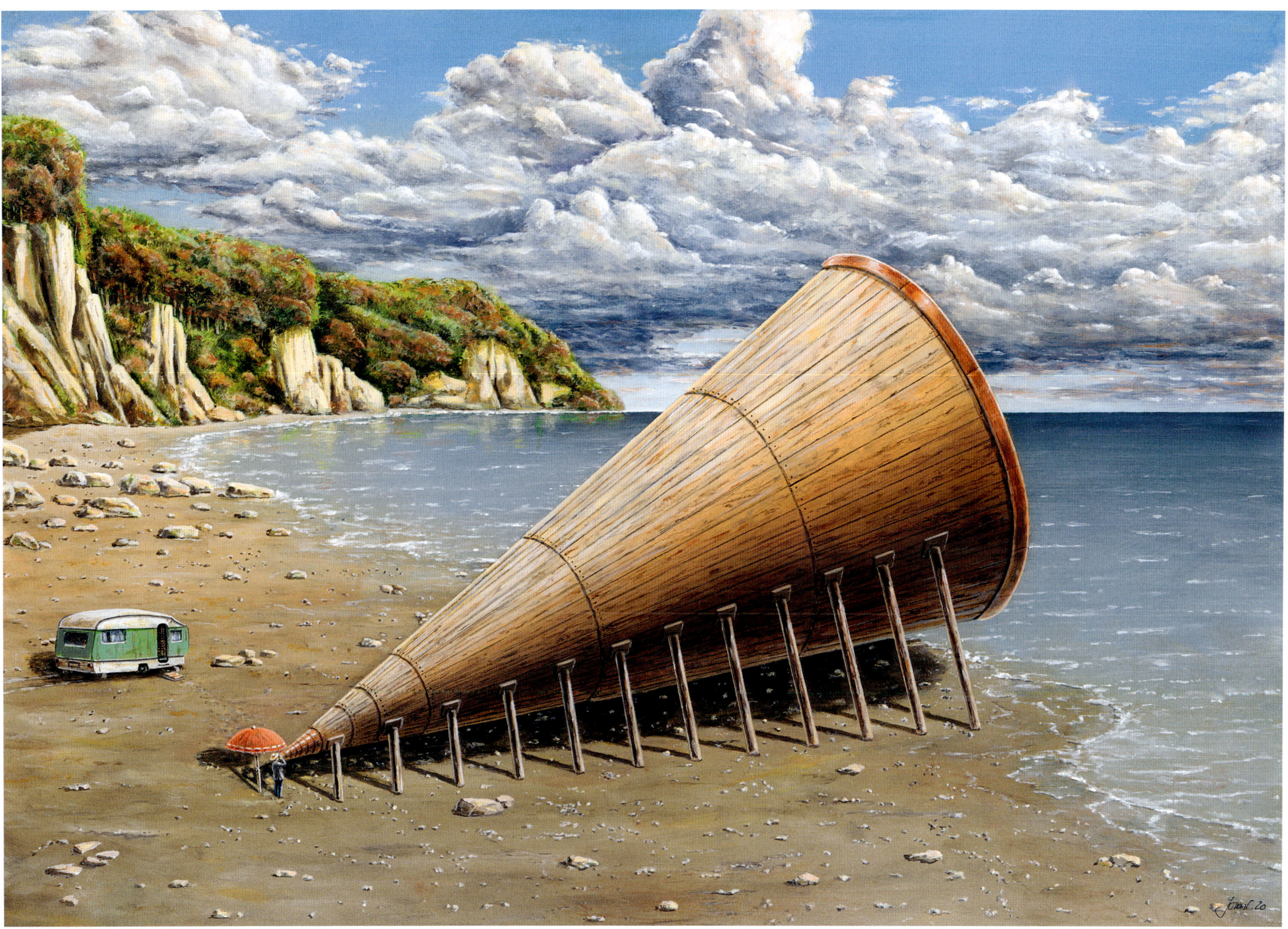

Meldestelle für nicht eingetroffene oder nicht fachgerecht ausgeführte Wunder

Reporting point for wonders that have not arrived or have not been carried out properly

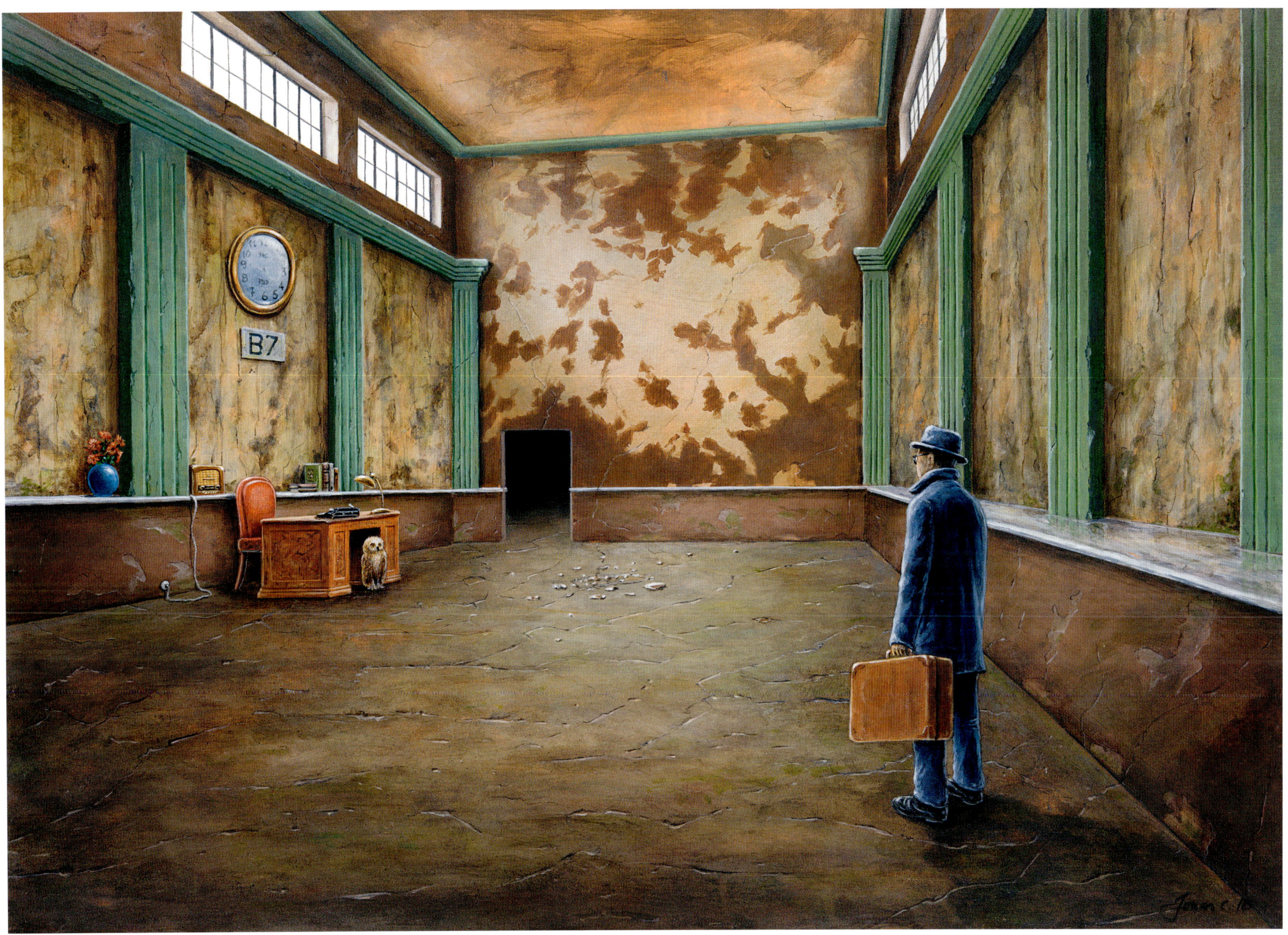
B7

Oskar Kaspar Lohmann, der vielleicht letzte
große Blechtrommler unserer Zeit

Oskar Kaspar Lohmann, perhaps the last
great tin drummer of our time

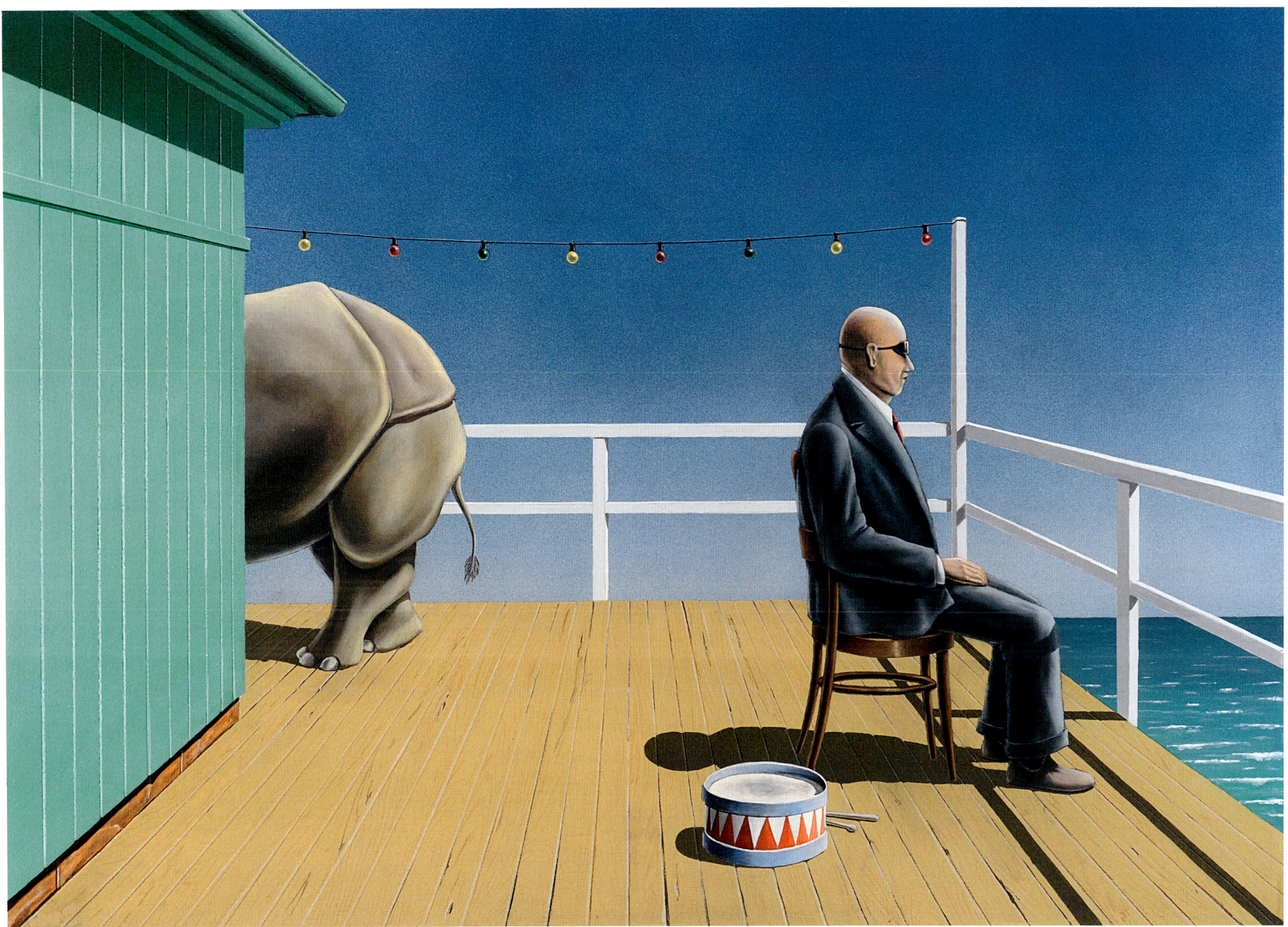

Das von den Gebrüdern Fellinirota erbaute »Marephono grande« in der Bucht von Massanazzo in Italien gehört seit 1967 zum Weltkulturerbe der UNESCO.

The "Marephono grande" in the bay of Massanazzo in Italy, built by the Fellinirota brothers, has been a UNESCO World Heritage Site since 1967.

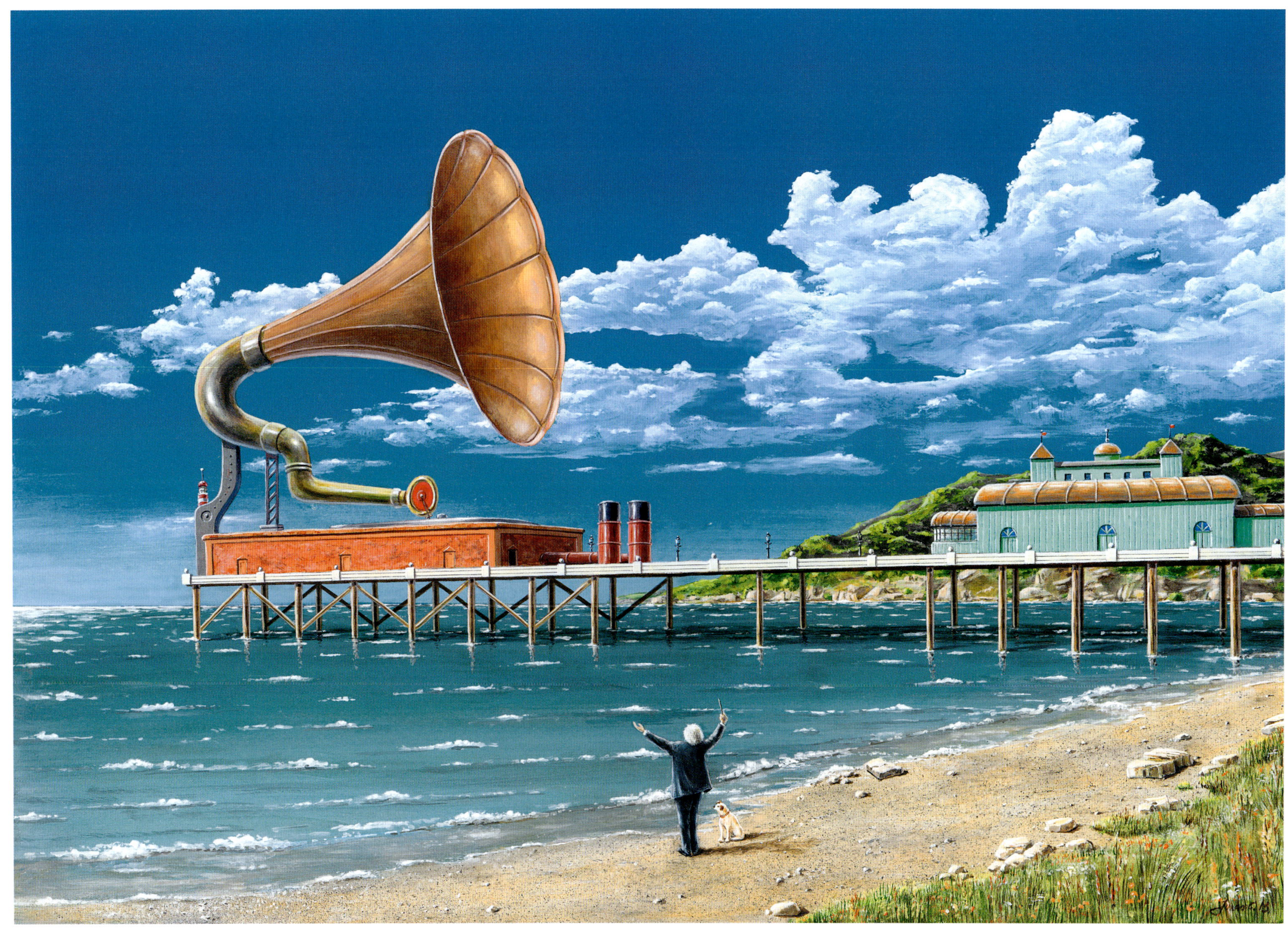

Der legendäre Oklahoma-Treck der großen
Landschnecken anno 1863

The legendary Oklahoma Trek of the great
land snails anno 1863

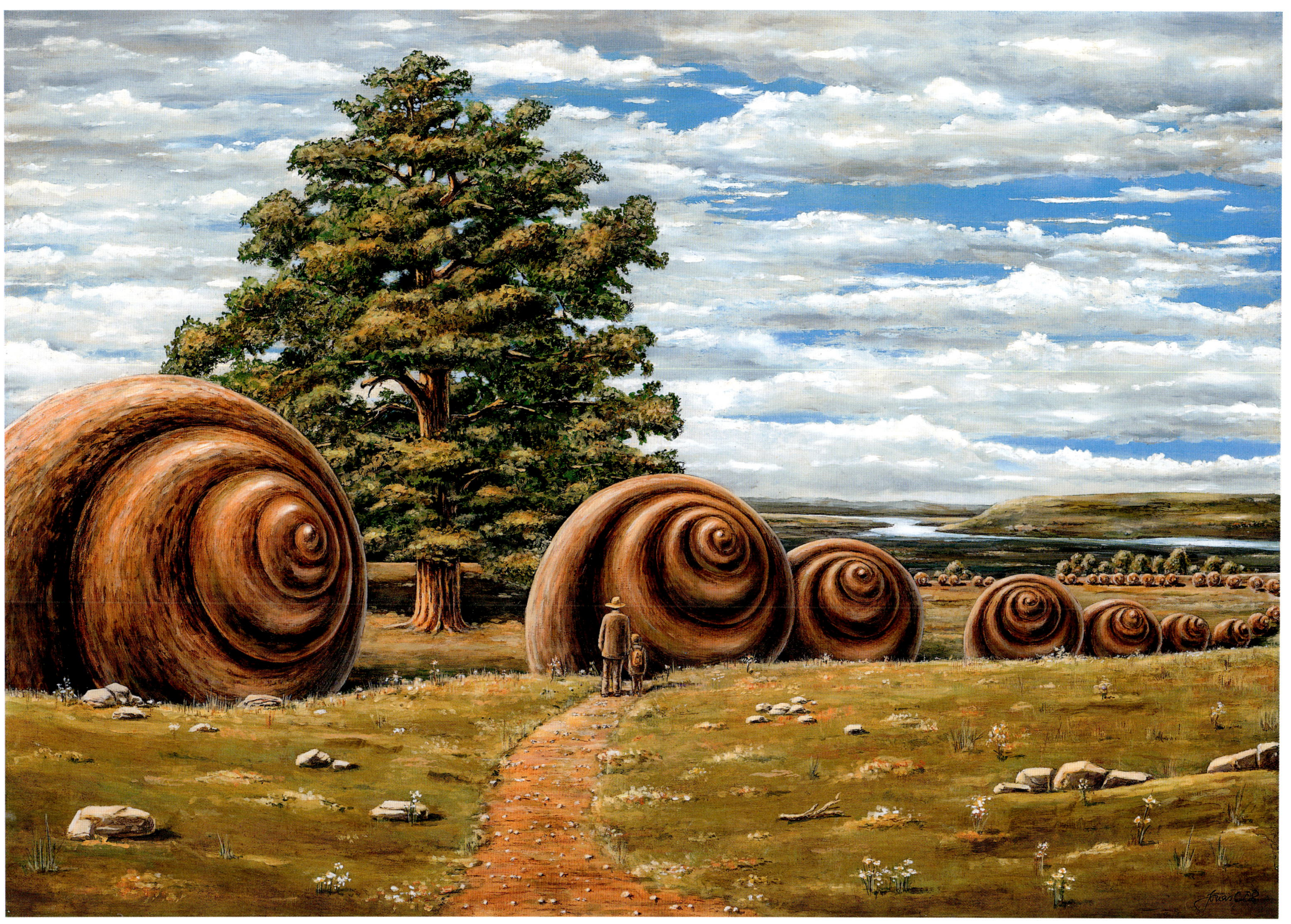

An diesem wunderschönen Sonntagmorgen entdeckte der kleine Albert ganz zufällig die Relativitätstheorie, welche viele, viele Jahre später das Verständnis von Raum und Zeit revolutionieren sollte und heute als Quantensprung der modernen Wissenschaft betrachtet wird, auch wenn Albert Einstein später einmal sagte: »*Seit die Mathematiker über die Relativitätstheorie hergefallen sind, verstehe ich sie selbst nicht mehr.*«

On this beautiful Sunday morning, little Albert discovered quite by accident the theory of relativity, which many, many years later was to revolutionize the understanding of space and time and today is regarded as a quantum leap in modern science, even if Albert Einstein later said: *"Since the mathematicians have fallen over the theory of relativity I no longer understand it myself."*

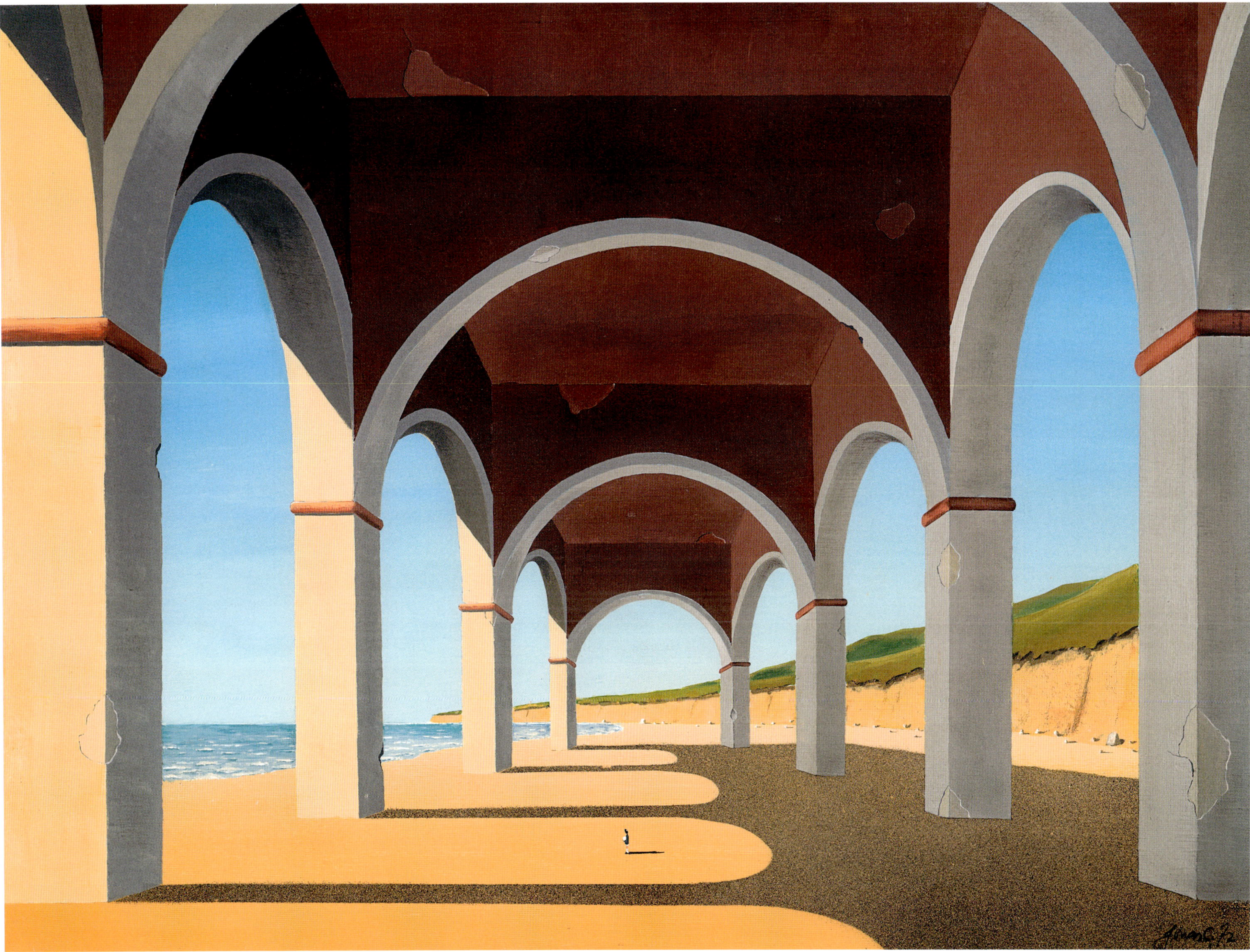

Gemeiner Steinfels (petralapis saxum divulgatus), Standort: Sonne bis Halbschatten, bis zur Blüte mäßig gießen und wöchentlich düngen. Verträgt keine Staunässe. Pflege: sehr anspruchsvoll.

Common stonecrop (petralapis saxum divulgatus), location: sun to partial shade, water moderately until flowering and fertilize weekly. Does not tolerate water stagnation. Care: very demanding.

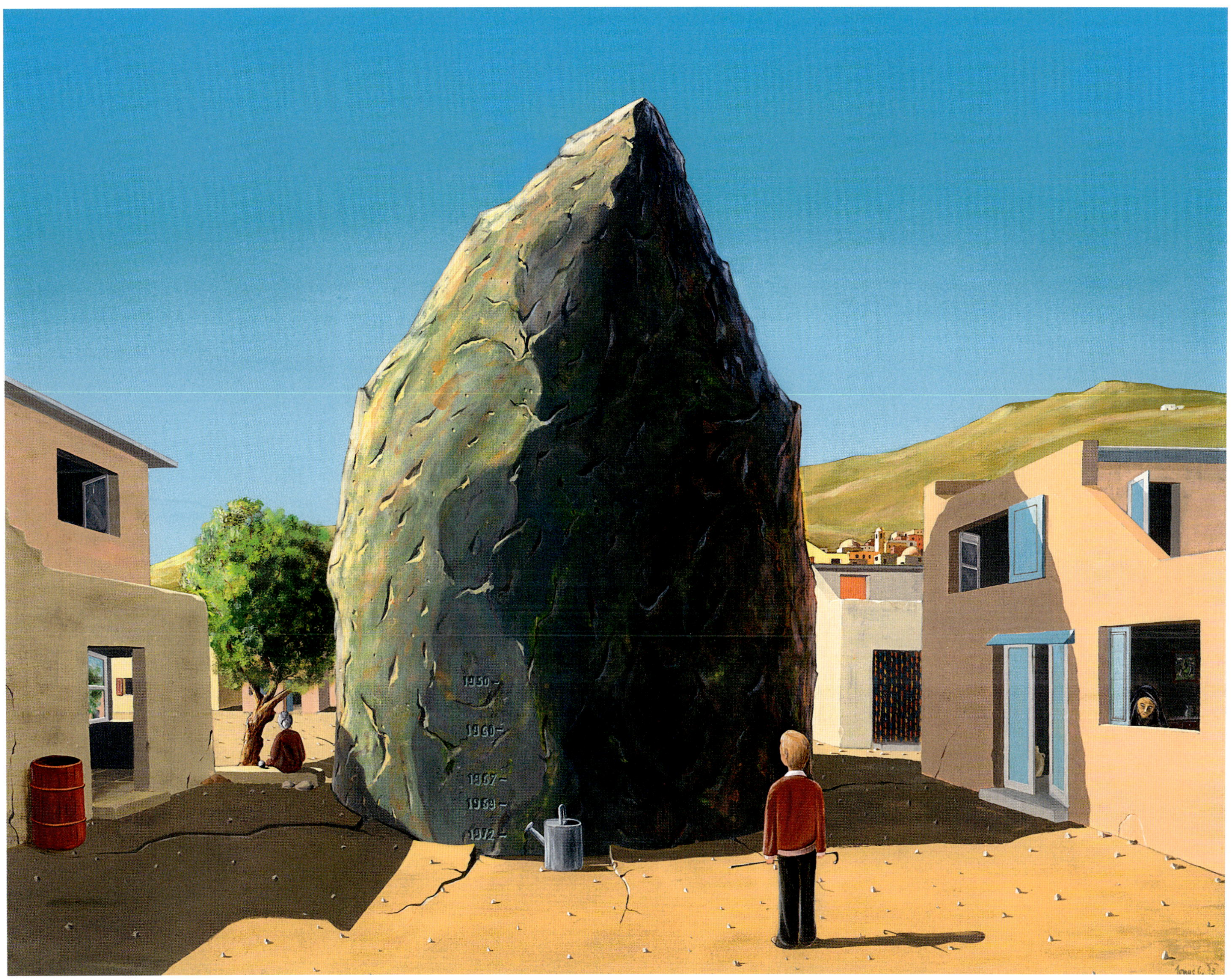

1950 –
1960 –
1967 –
1969 –
1972 –

<u>2002</u>

Dem »Zeppallon« sagen Fachleute eine große
Zukunft voraus und es gilt als unbestritten,
dass er die zivile Luftfahrt in den nächsten
Jahren vollkommen revolutionieren wird.

Experts predict a great future for the
"Zeppallon" and it is considered undisputed,
that it will completely revolutionize civil
aviation in the coming years.

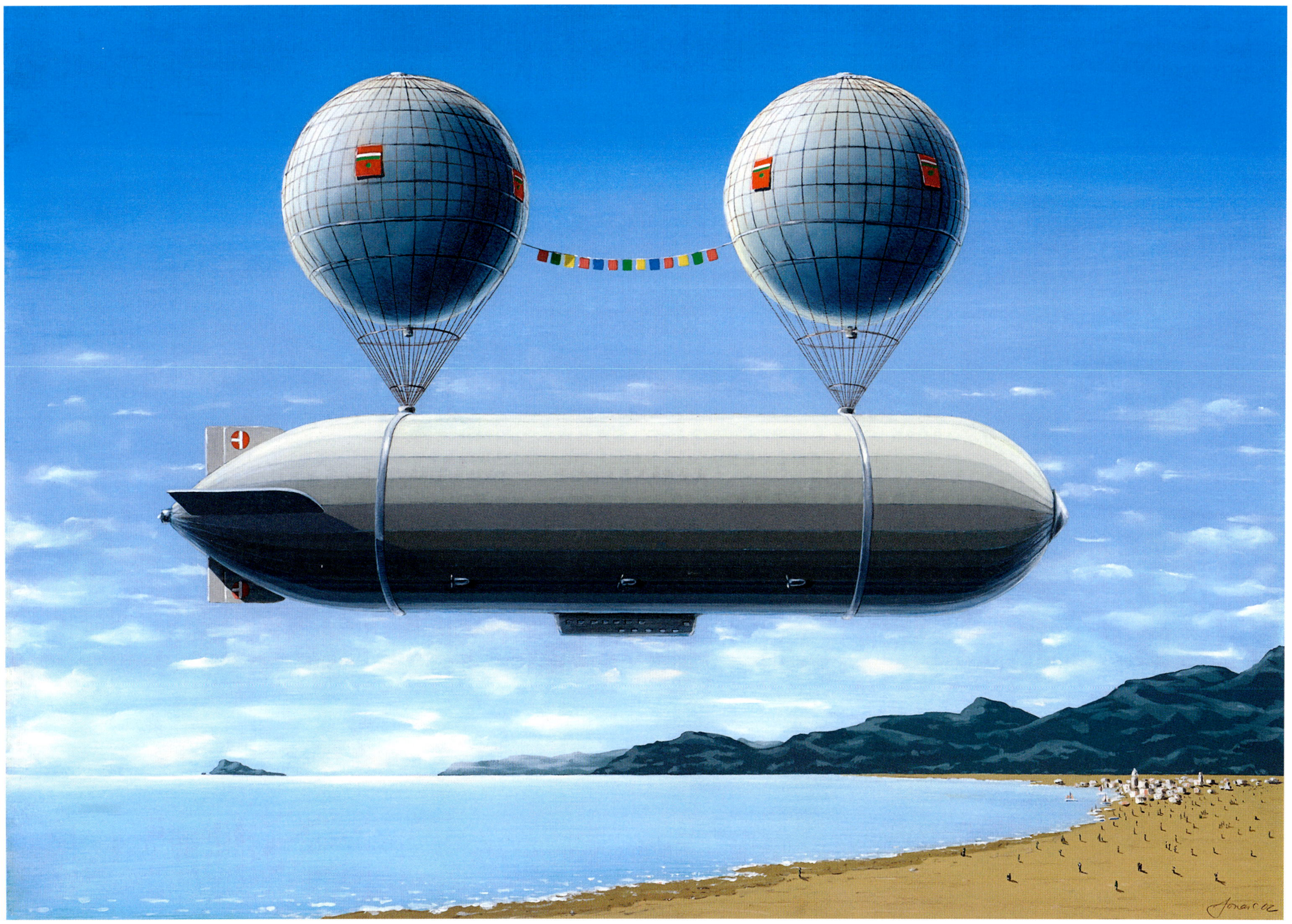

Die Angst der Schnecke vor dem Sprung
oder Wo ein Wille ist, ist auch ein Weg,
aber alles braucht seine Zeit

The snail's fear of the leap or
Where there is a will, there is a way,
but everything takes time

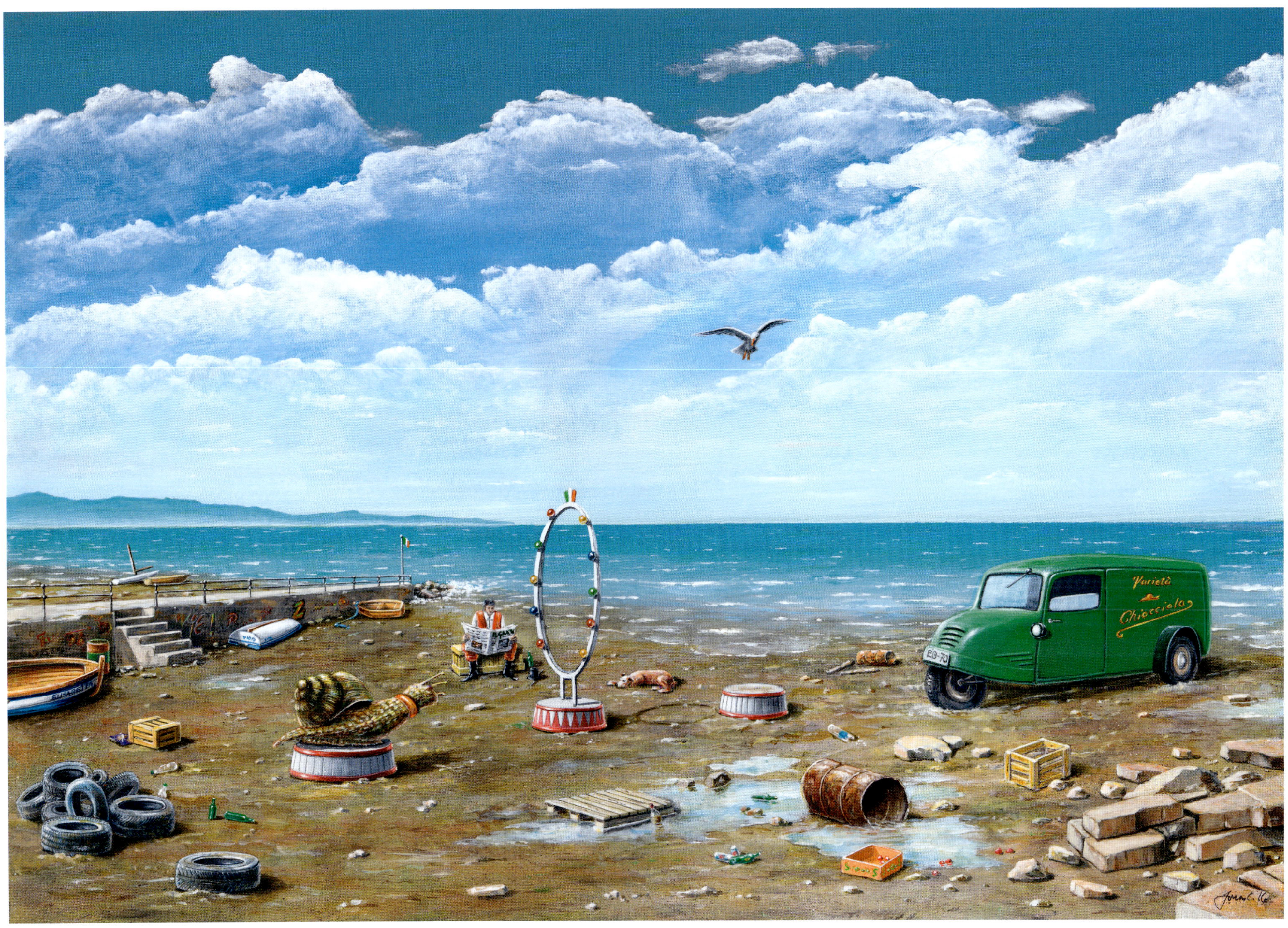

Varietà
Chiocciola

**Die großen Gefühle einer
verliebten Schildkröte**

The great feelings of
a turtle in love

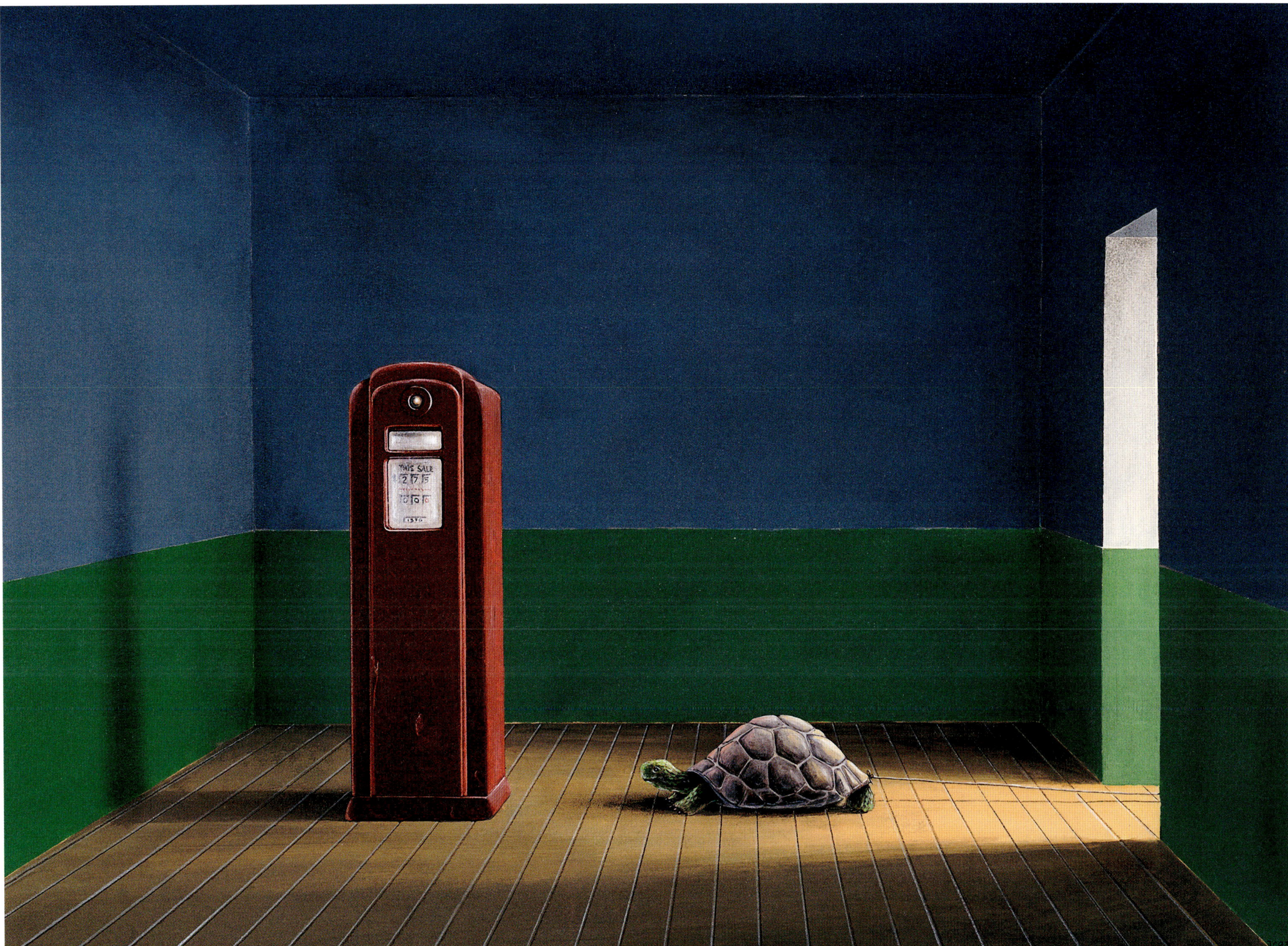

THIS SALE
2 7 5
0 0 0
1370

Gemeinsames Meditieren macht Freude
und weckt ungeahnte Kräfte

Meditating together brings joy
and awakens undreamt-of powers

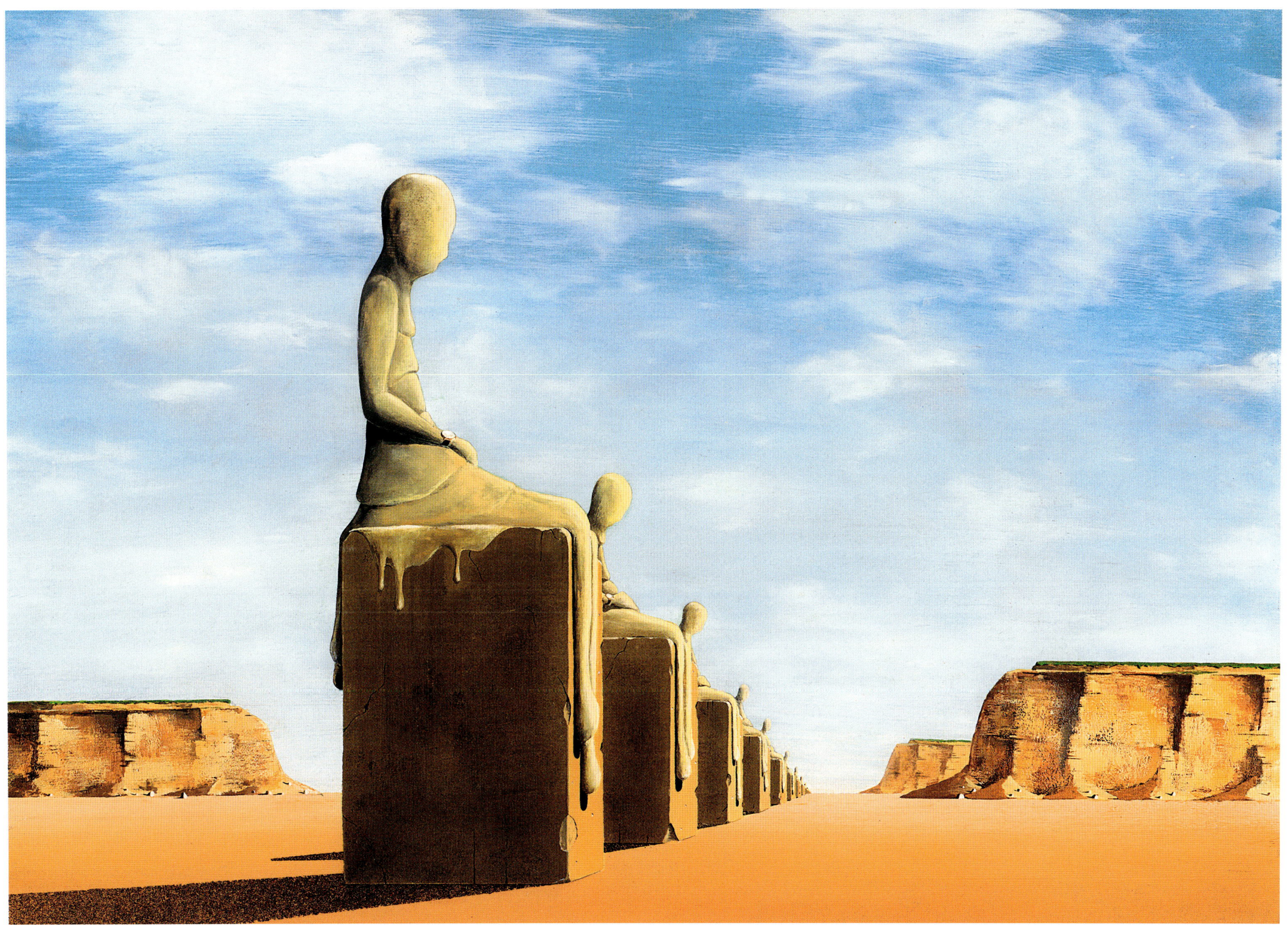

Es war einmal vor langer, langer Zeit
ein Traumforscher, ein gewisser Sigismund
Schlomo Freud, welcher glaubte, dass
*»Träume nichts anderes sind, als eine
Befriedigung eines verdrängten Trieb-
wunsches und sie intime Botschaften aus
der Kindheit enthalten«.*

Once upon a time, long, long ago there
was a dream researcher, a certain
Sigismund Schlomo Freud, who believed
that *"dreams are nothing more than the
satisfaction of a repressed urge and they
contain intimate messages from childhood".*

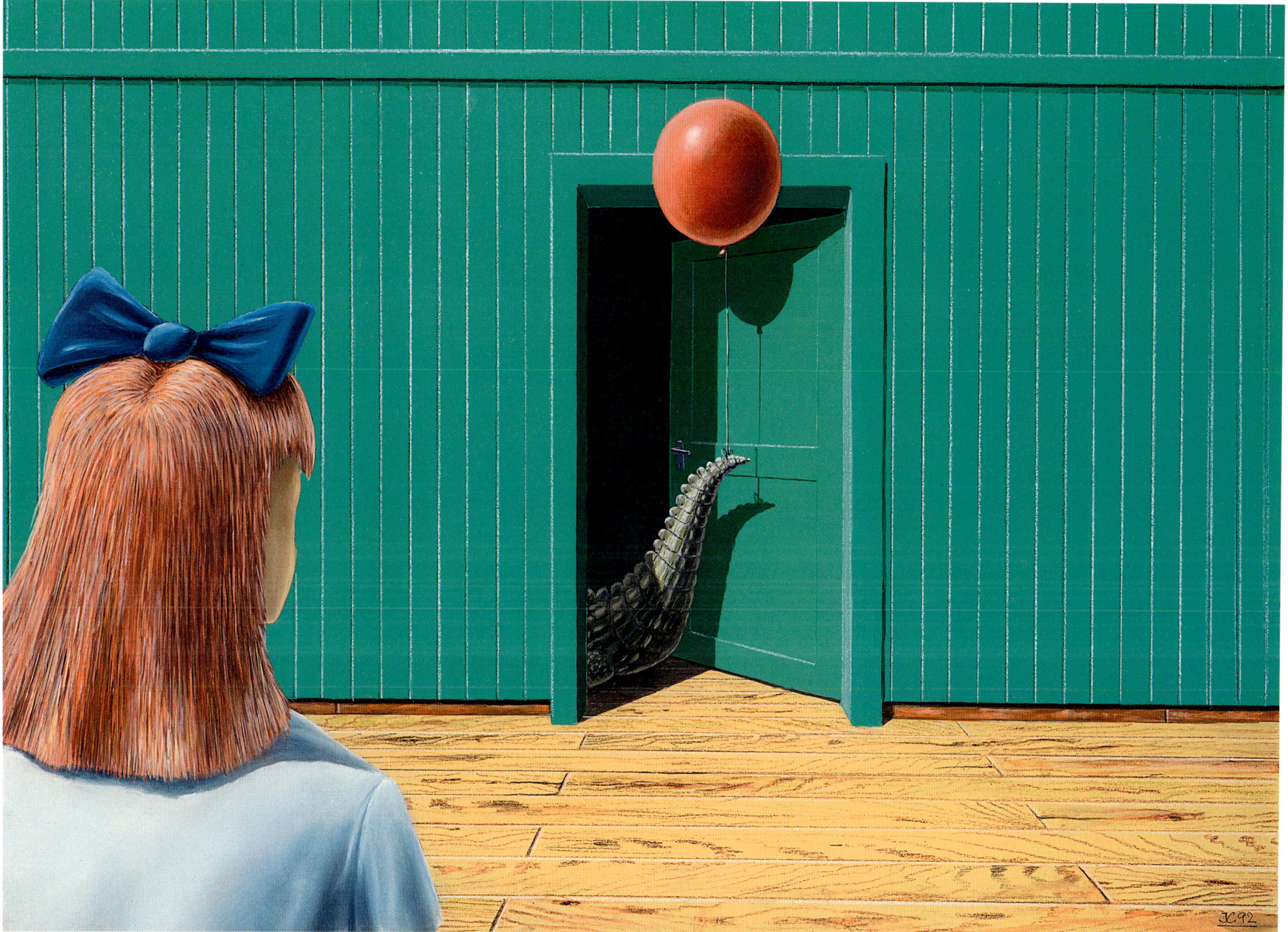

<u>1983</u>

**Ein gefundenes Fressen
für Psychoanalytiker**

A found food
for psychoanalysts

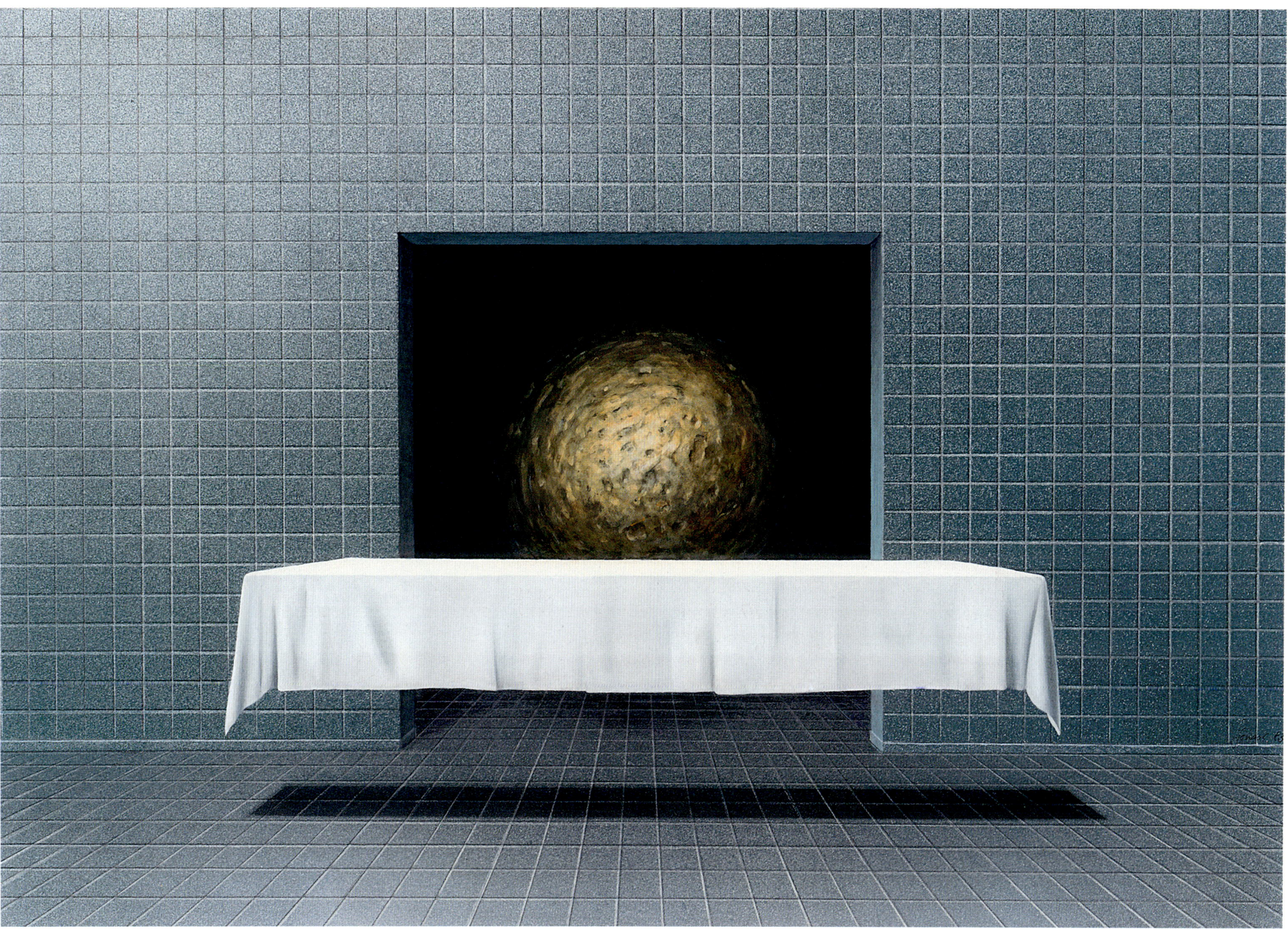

Die Leichtigkeit eines Traums oder
Schwere Träume sind in der Regel
nicht schwerer als leichte Träume,
aber wesentlich nachhaltiger

The lightness of a dream or
Heavy dreams are usually
not heavier than light dreams,
but much more lasting

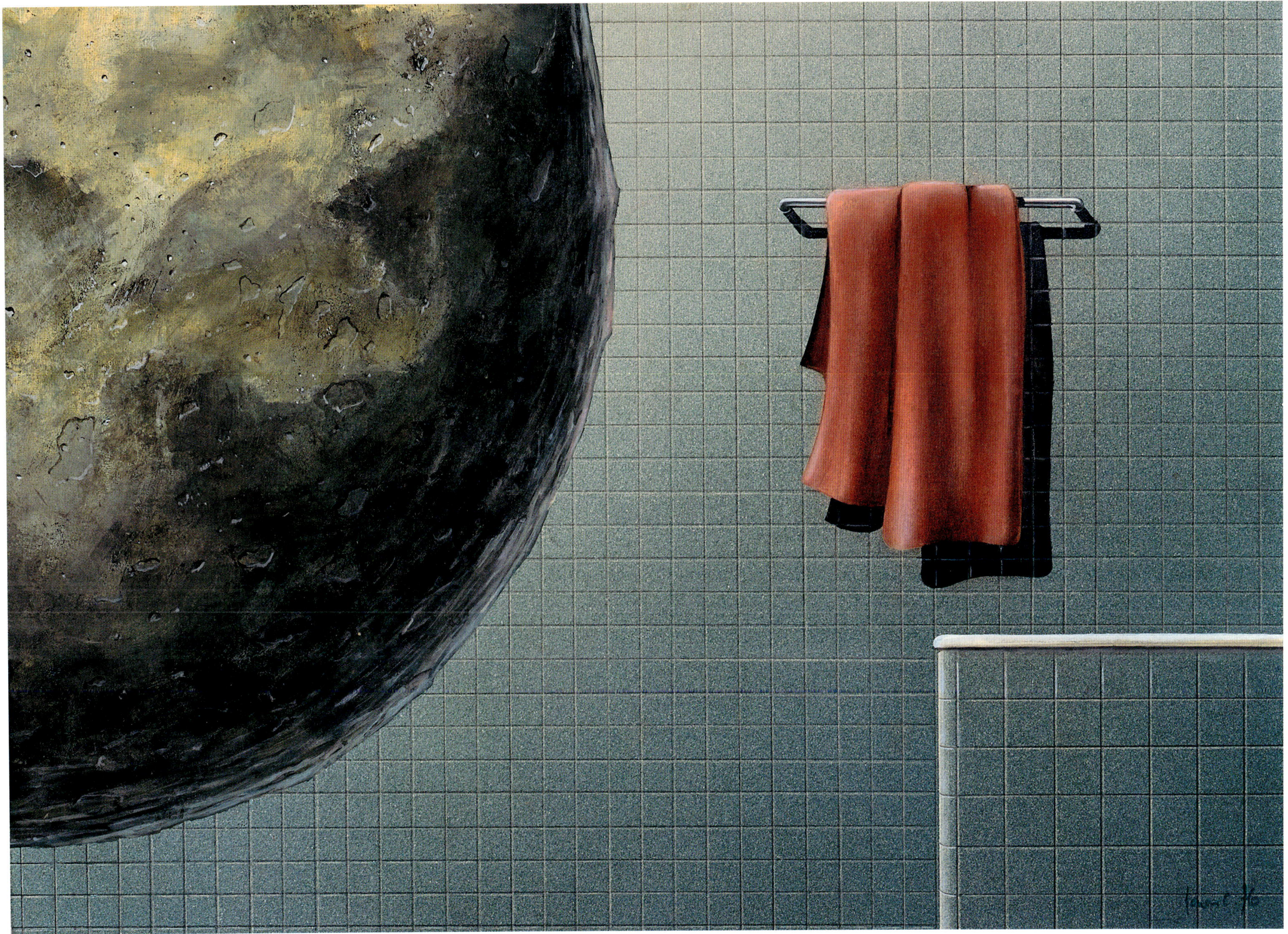

Der Asteroid AL413C von der Größe eines kleinen Einfamilienhauses, stürzte am 28.3.2019 um 15:04 Ortszeit nicht wie von den Raumfahrtbehörden vorausgesagt in den südlichen Pazifik, sondern in eine kleine Pfütze außerhalb der Industriestadt Raunitz. Damit hatte niemand gerechnet, auch nicht Fridolin Holzinger, welcher hier seit seiner Pensionierung jeden Tag fischte, immer begleitet von seinem treuen Freund Kater Schubert, genannt »Schubi«.

The asteroid AL413C, the size of a small family home, crashed on 3.28.2019 at 3:04 pm local time not into the southern Pacific Ocean as predicted by the space authorities, but into a small puddle outside the industrial town of Raunitz. Nobody had expected this, not even Fridolin Holzinger, who had been fishing here every day since his retirement, always accompanied by his faithful friend Schubert the cat, called "Schubi".

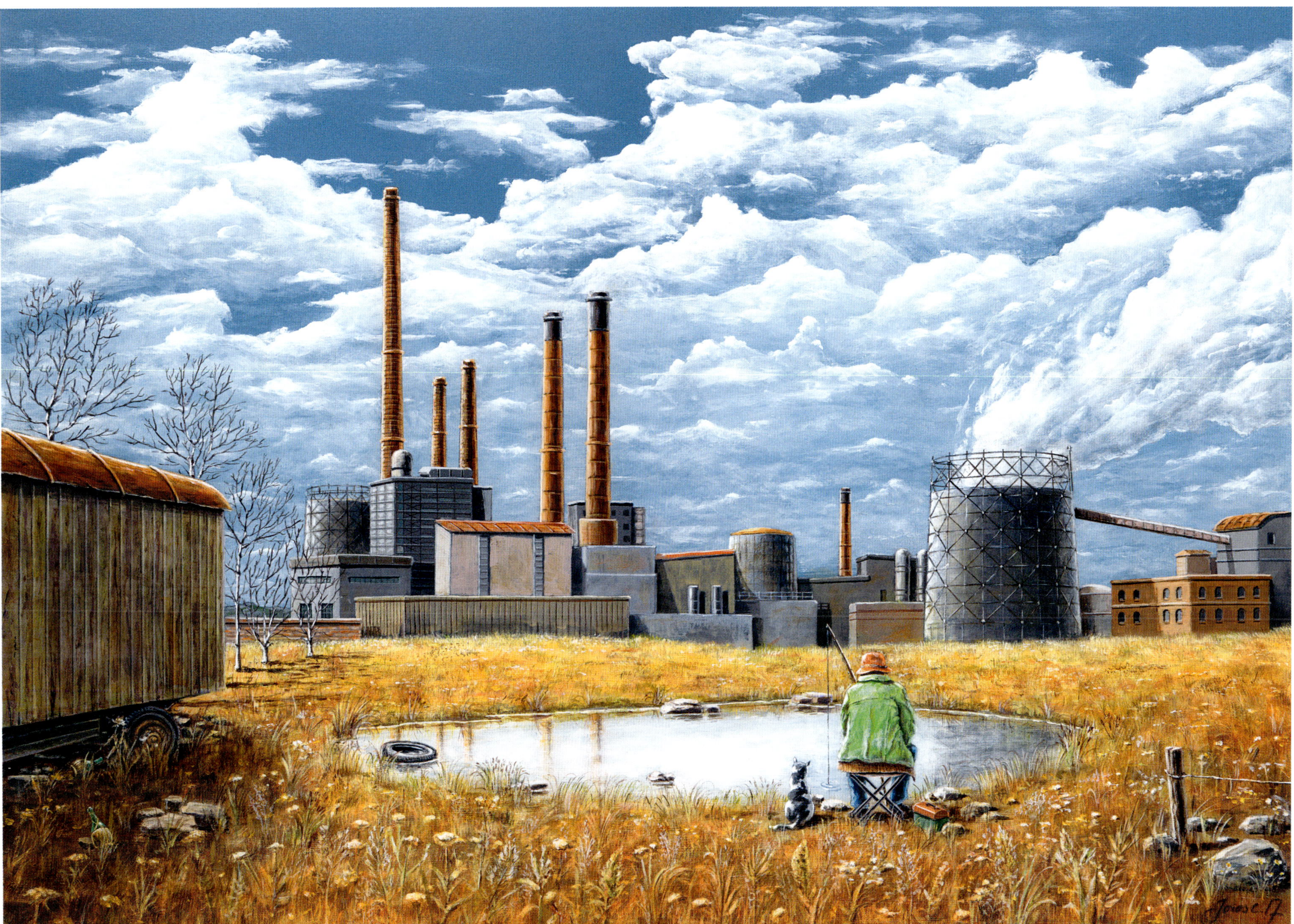

<u>2021</u>

Alice und Bernadette im Wunderland   Alice and Bernadette in Wonderland

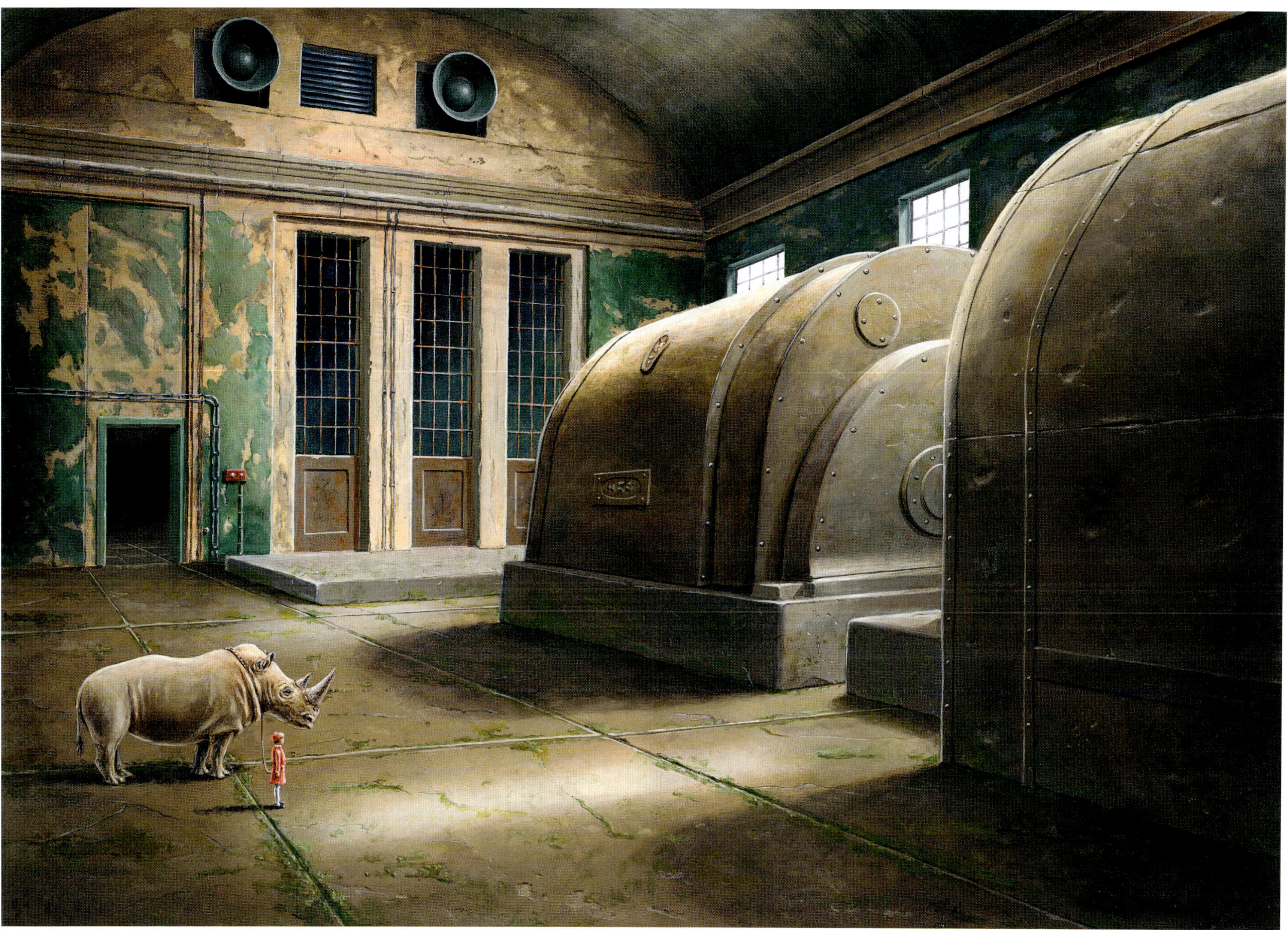

Die angekündigte, aber doch etwas seltsame
Verwandlung des Landvermessers Franz K.

The announced, yet somewhat strange
transformation of the surveyor Franz K.

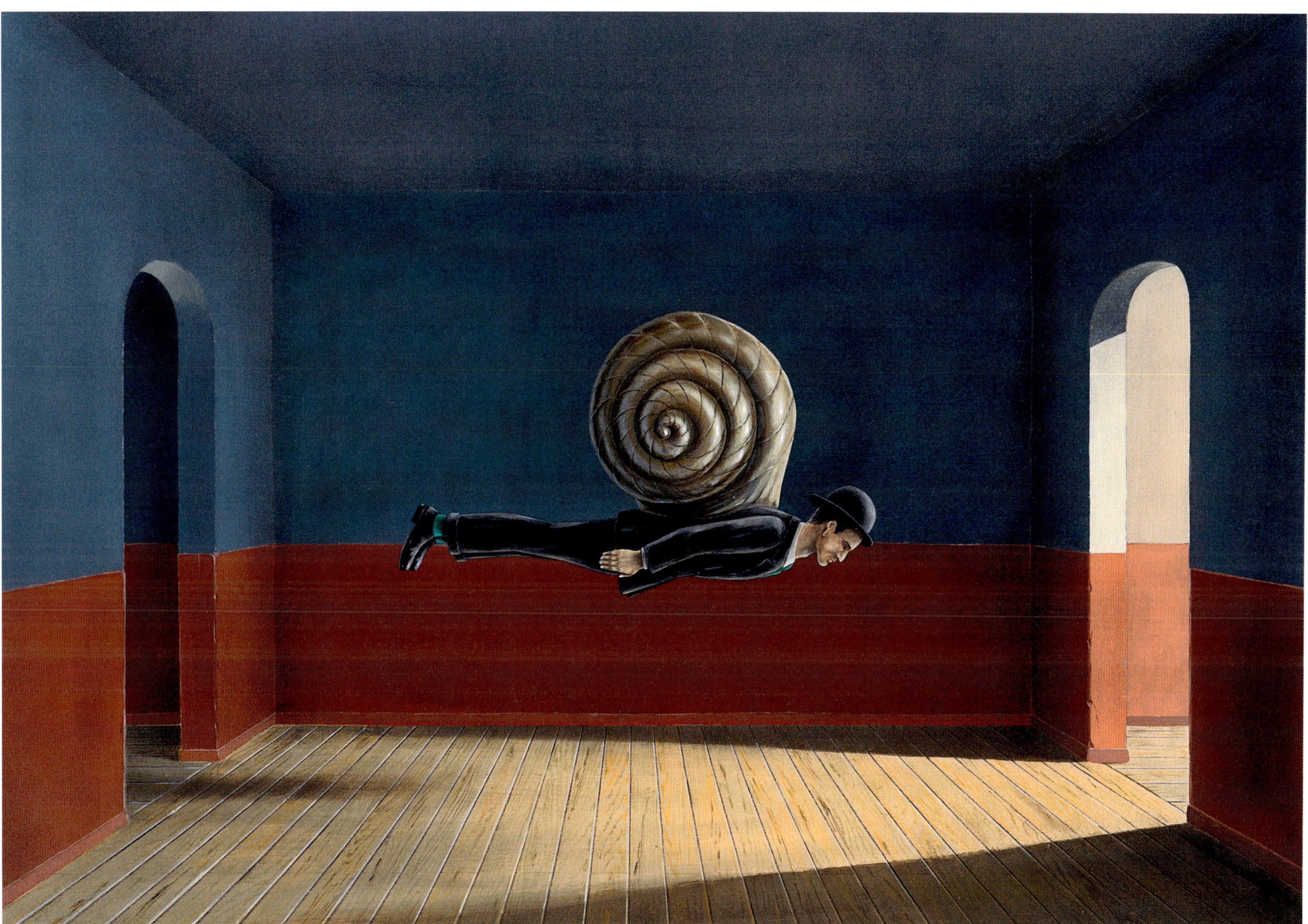

Sir Carson Elgar Albee 1938–2012, englischer Schriftsteller, schrieb viele weltbekannte Bestseller wie »Die Einsamkeit des Regentropfens«, »Die unglaubliche, aber wahre Geschichte der außerordentlich hässlichen Meerjungfrau«, »Der Schatten des Glühwurms« sowie den Kinderbuchklassiker »Egon, der Fisch, der nicht wasserdicht war«. Weniger bekannt ist, dass er auch die Drehbücher zur legendären Trickfilmserie »Speedy Buddha and the Groovy Pope« schrieb, der weltweit erfolgreichsten Trickfilmserie aller Zeiten.

Sir Carson Elgar Albee 1938–2012, English writer, wrote many world-famous bestsellers such as "The Loneliness of the Raindrop", "The Incredible but True Story of the Extraordinarily Ugly Mermaid", "The Glowworm's Shadow", as well as the classic children's book "Egon, the Fish That Wasn't Waterproof". Less well known is that he also wrote the scripts for the legendary animated series "Speedy Buddha and the Groovy Pope", the world's most successful animated series of all time.

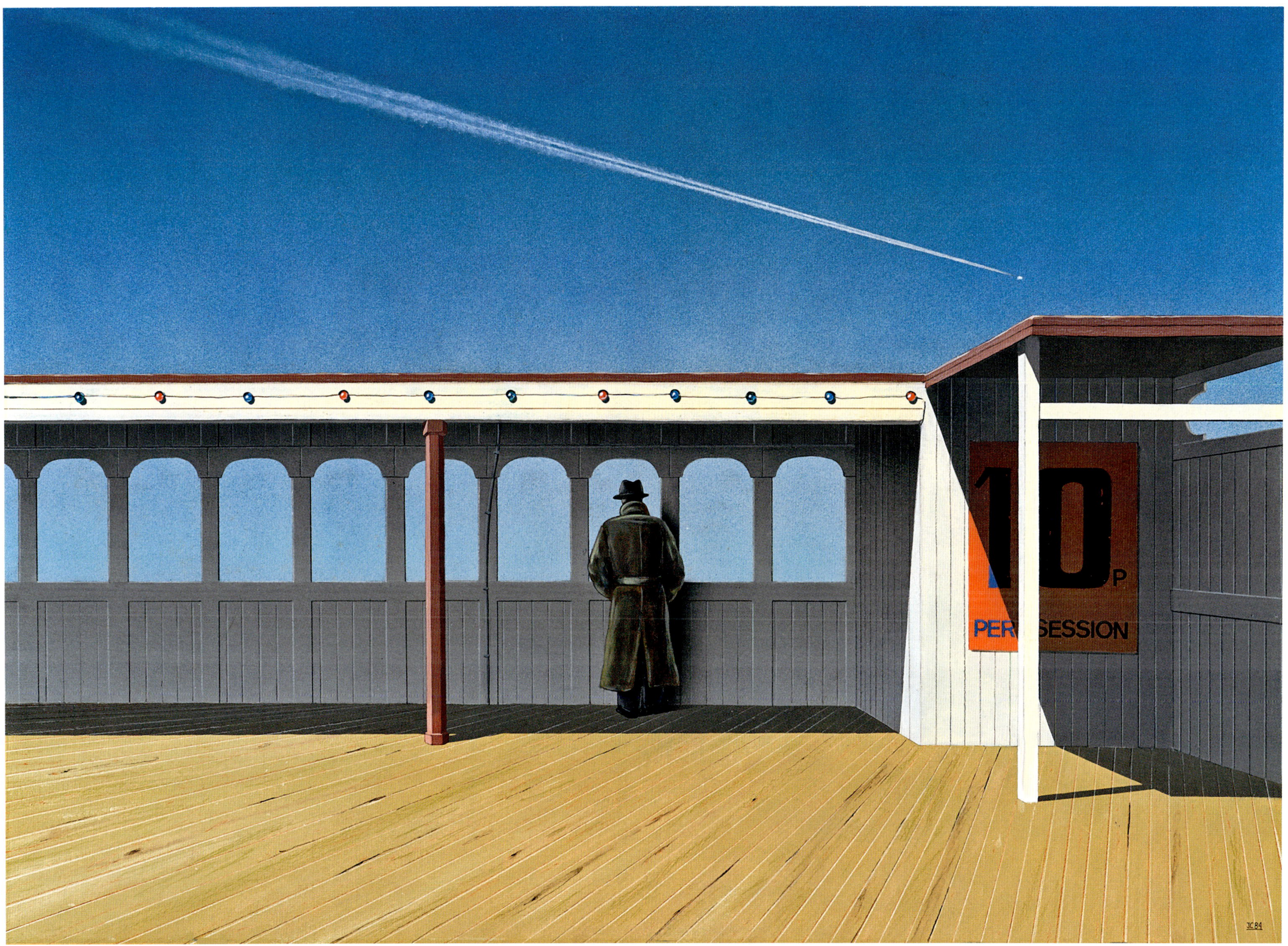

10p
PER SESSION

Die siebte Realität oder Die verschiedenen
Ebenen des Lebens – man muss sich nur
für die richtige entscheiden

The seventh reality or The different levels of
life – you just have to choose the right one

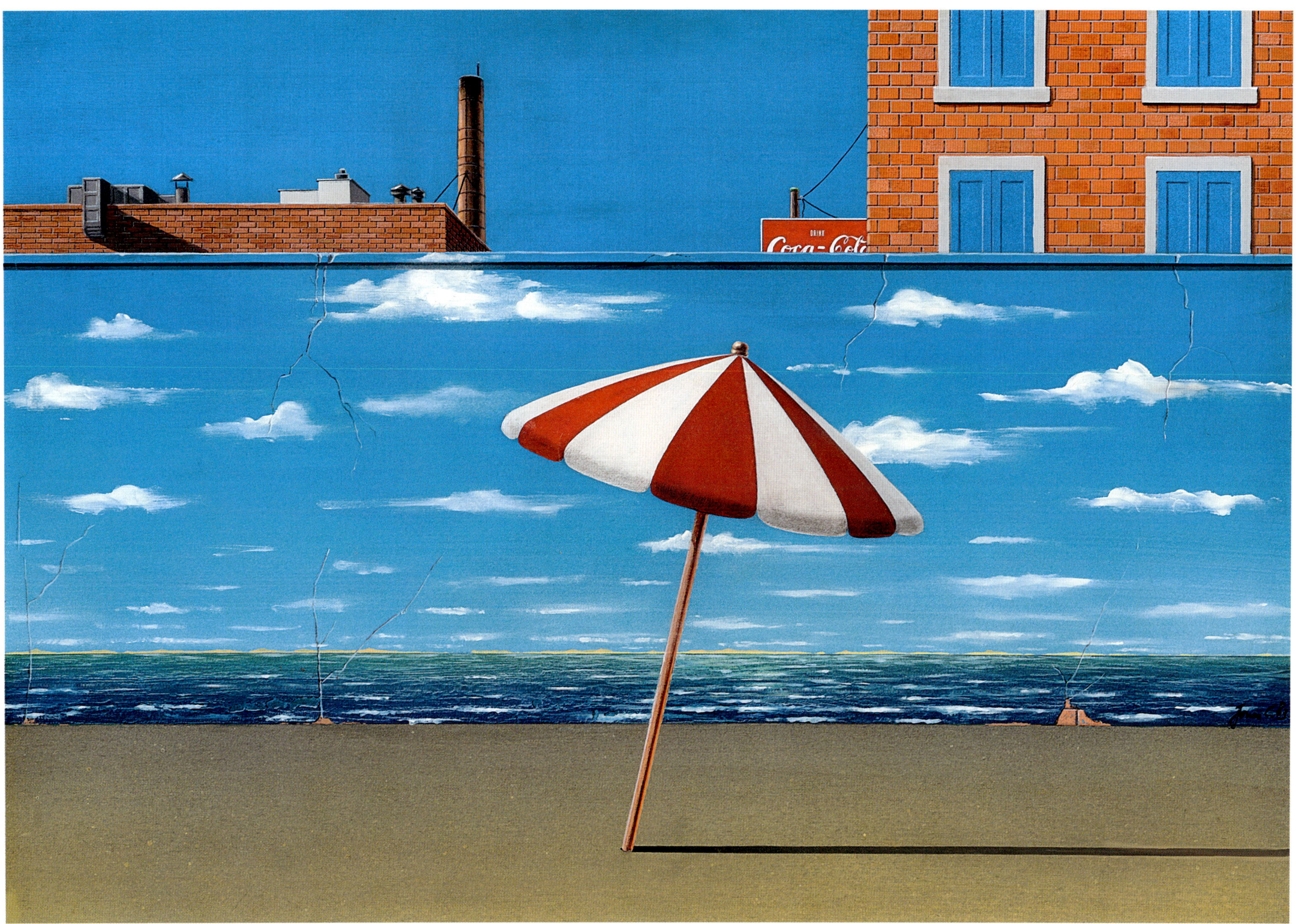

DRINK
Coca-Cola

**Elefantasien oder die heimlichen Sehnsüchte
eines leicht schwermütigen Dickhäuters**

Elefantasies or the secret longings of
a slightly melancholy pachyderm

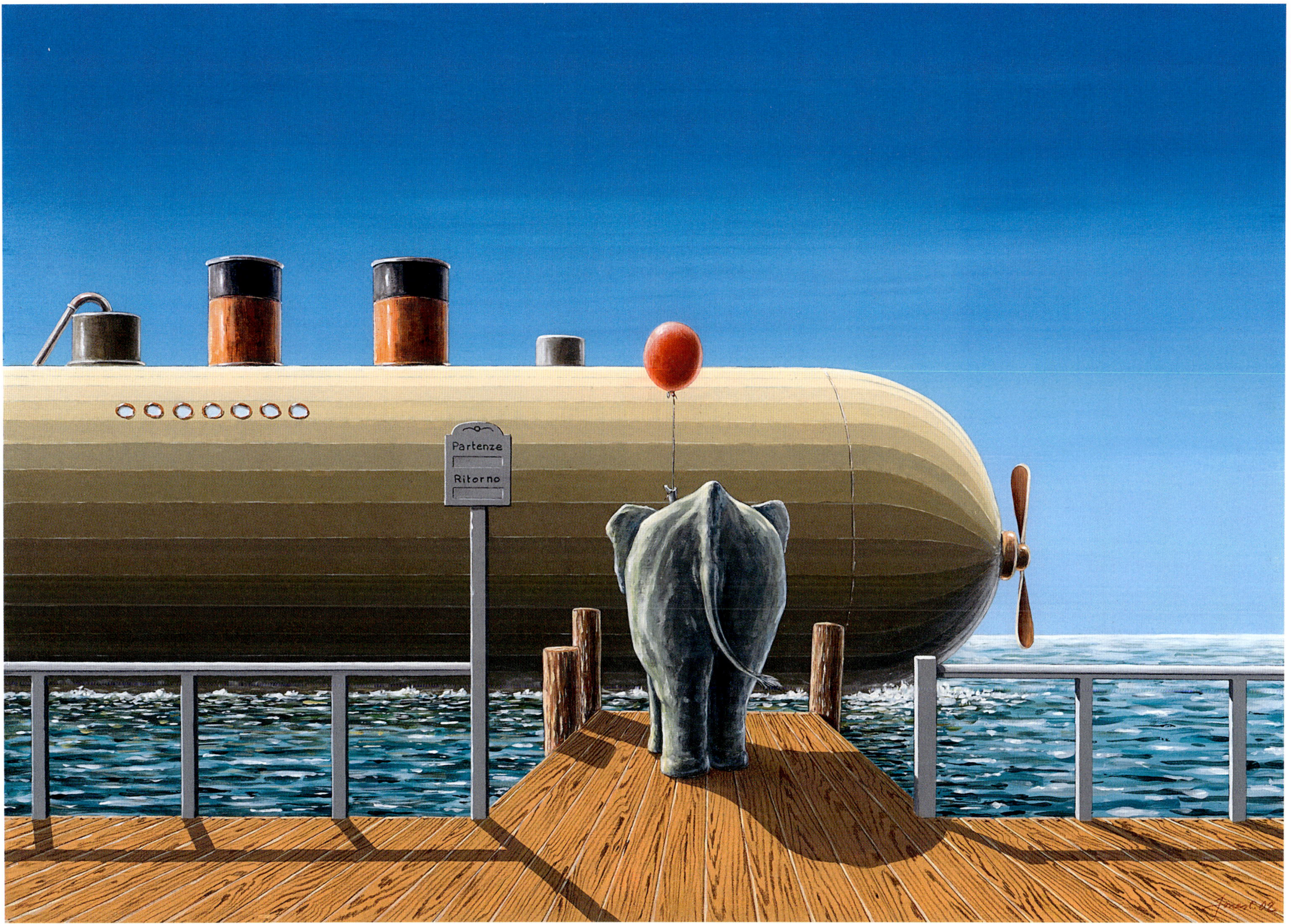

Partenze
Ritorno

Kaum ein anderes Lebewesen hat sich so perfekt der hochalpinen Umgebung angepasst wie die spitzohrige Bergschildkröte. Sie ist eine flinke Kletterin, verfügt über eine erstaunliche Sprungkraft und ist dank ihres praktisch unzerstörbaren Panzers eine ausgezeichnete Gleiterin auf Schnee und Eis. Zudem übersteht sie Lawinenniedergänge vollkommen unbeschadet und Stürze in Gletscherspalten können ihr nichts anhaben, da sie die Fähigkeit hat, sich in einen jahrzehntelangen Winterschlaf zu versetzen. Weibliche Exemplare dieser einzigartigen Spezies können bis zu 120 Jahr alt werden.

Hardly any other creature has adapted so perfectly to the high alpine environment as the pointed-eared mountain tortoise. It is a nimble climber, has amazing jumping power and, thanks to its practically indestructible shell, is an excellent glider on snow and ice. In addition, it survives avalanches completely unscathed and falls into crevasses cannot harm it, as it has the ability to hibernate for decades. Females of this unique species can live up to 120 years.

Hommage an Robert Haefeli, Glaziologe
und Polarforscher (1898–1978)

Homage to Robert Haefeli, glaciologist
and polar explorer (1898–1978)

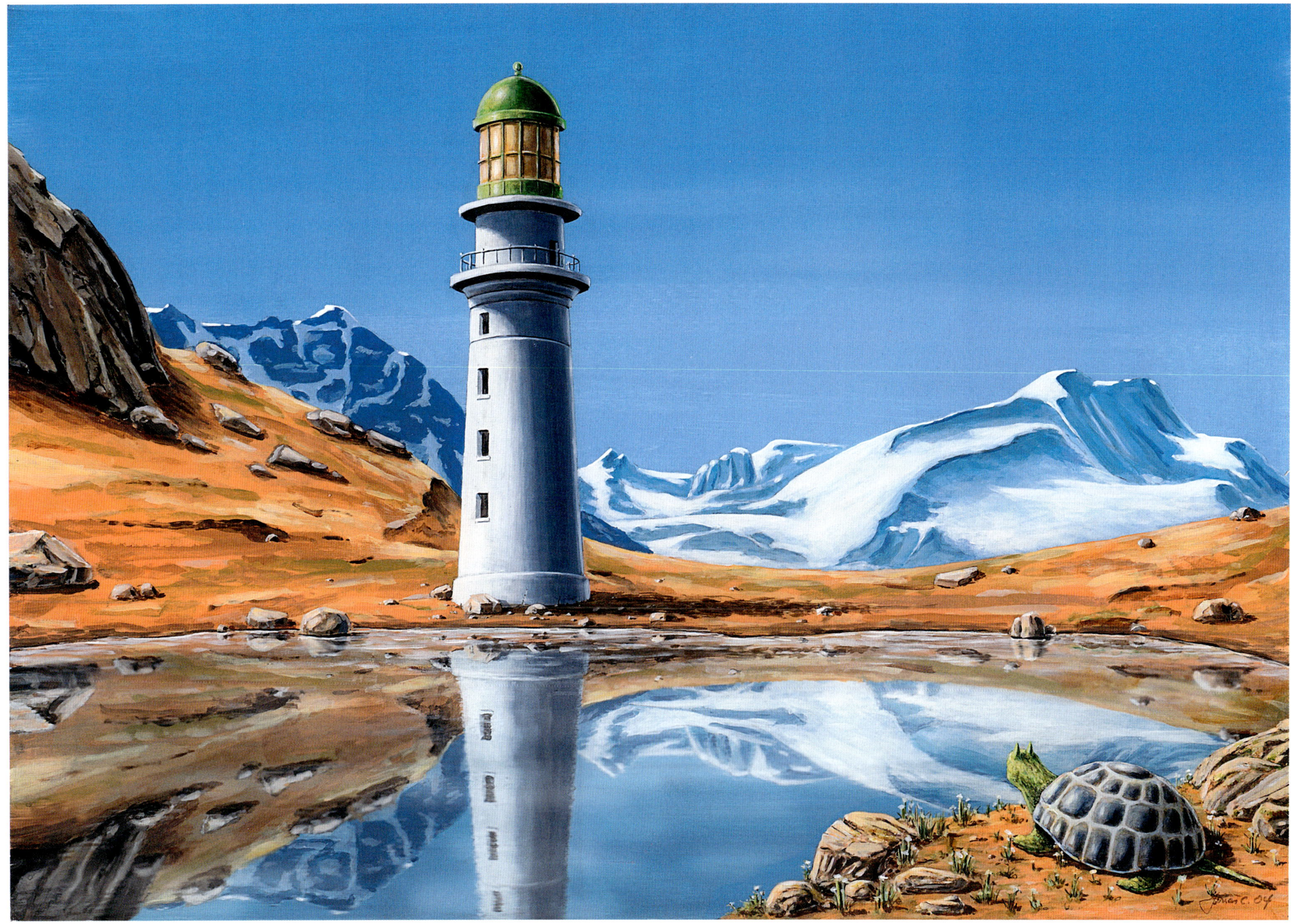

Elwood Allan Gorey ist überzeugt,
nur in der Fantasie seiner Mitmenschen
zu existieren.

Elwood Allan Gorey is convinced
that he exists only in the imagination
of his fellow men.

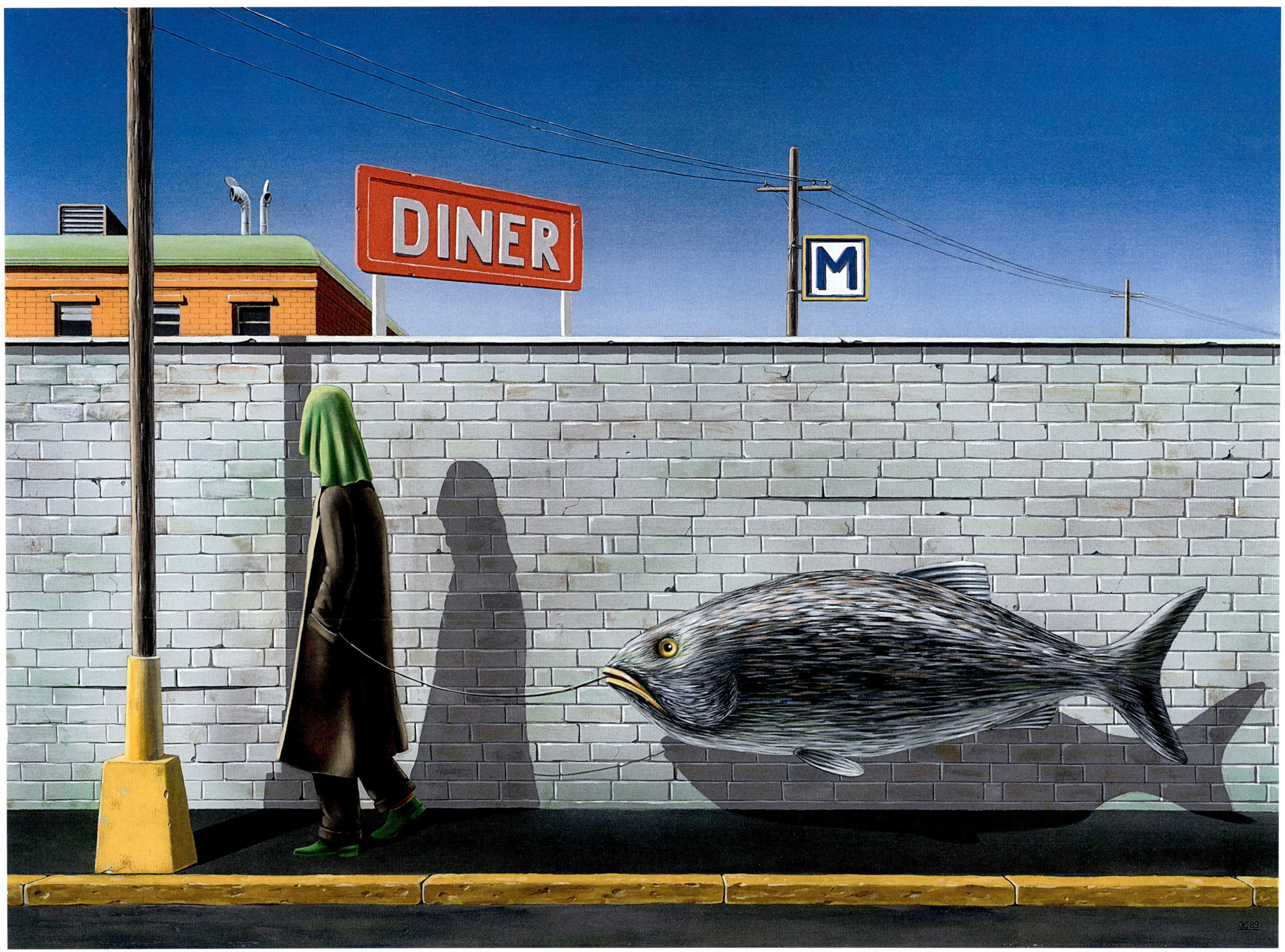

DINER
M

Die traurige Ballade vom verwirrten Taucher,
der das Meer nicht mehr fand

The sad ballad of the confused diver
who could no longer find the sea

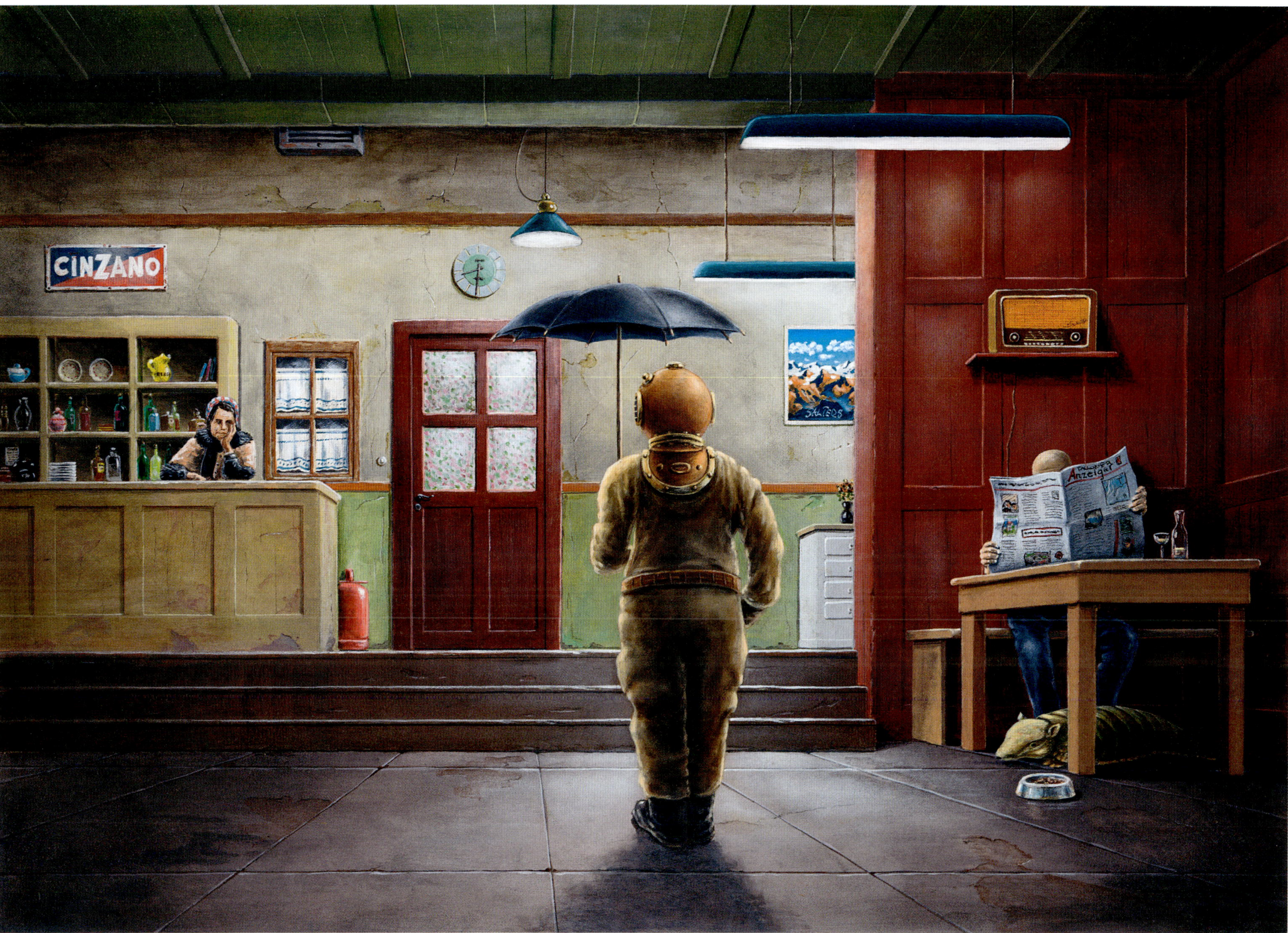

CINZANO
Anzeiger

Die wundersamen Abenteuer des kleinen
Sebastian, der eigentlich nur Schmetterlinge
fangen wollte

The wondrous adventures of little Sebastian,
who really only wanted to catch butterflies

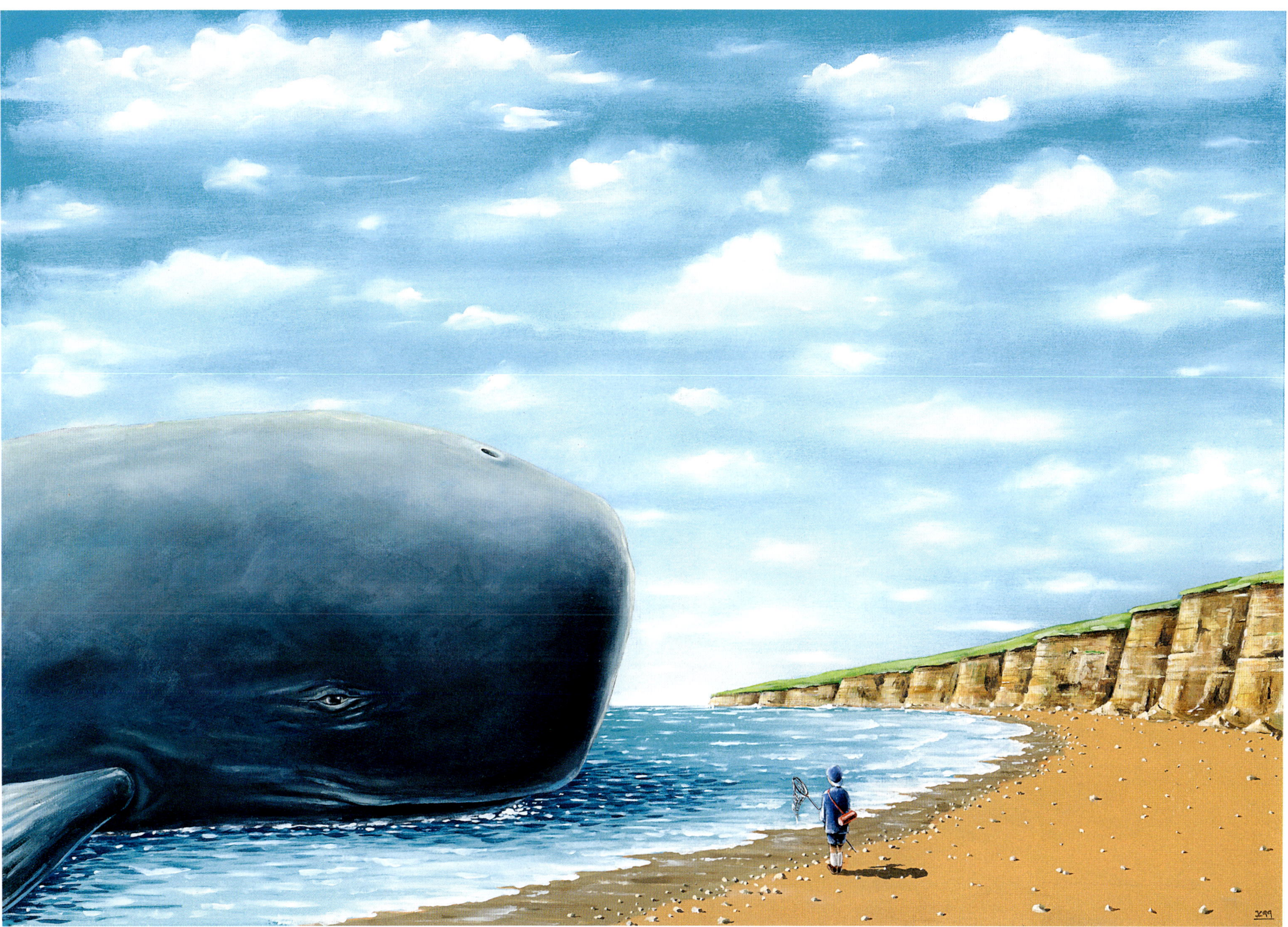

Eine außerordentlich prächtige, männliche
»malacosoma quercifolia verdis«.
Die Weibchen werden bis zu siebenmal
größer und fressen ihre männlichen Artge-
nossen noch vor der Paarung auf, was
zumindest in der Tierwelt einmalig ist.
Über die Bedeutung dieses Verhaltens weiß
man nichts Genaues. Heute gibt es nur
noch wenige, vereinzelte Exemplare dieser
urtümlichen Kopffüßer.

An exceptionally magnificent male
"malacosoma quercifolia verdis".
The females grow up to seven times
and eat their male conspecifics even
before mating which is unique at least
in the animal world. Nothing is known
about the meaning of this behavior.
Today, only a few isolated specimens of
these primitive cephalopods remain.

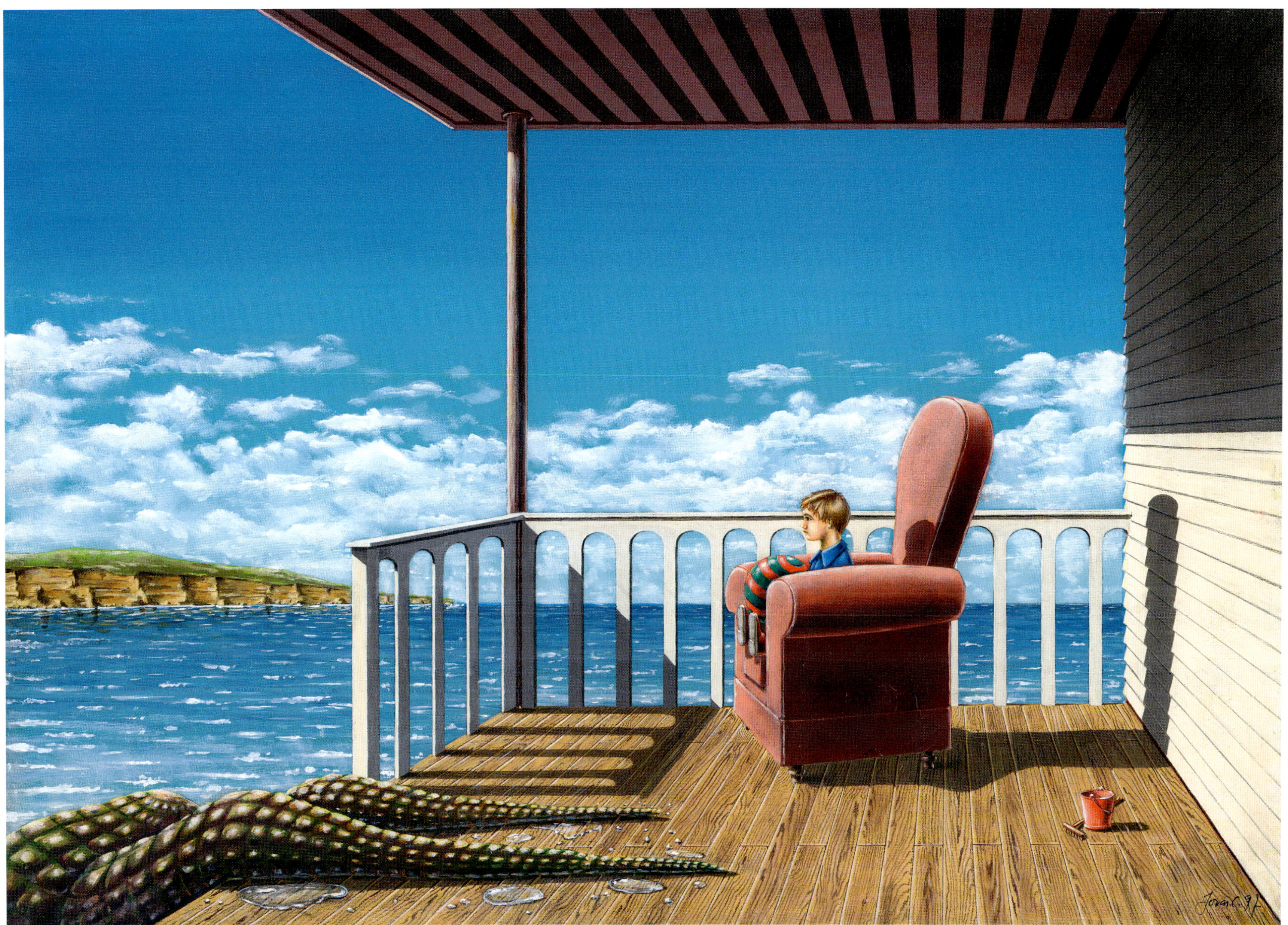

Mit seiner wissenschaftlichen
Abhandlung »Das afrikanische Nashorn
im öffentlich-rechtlichen Raum«
erregte Ferdinand Borchert-Strohmeier
internationales Aufsehen.

With his scientific treatise
"The African rhinoceros in public law"
Ferdinand Borchert-Strohmeier
caused an international sensation.

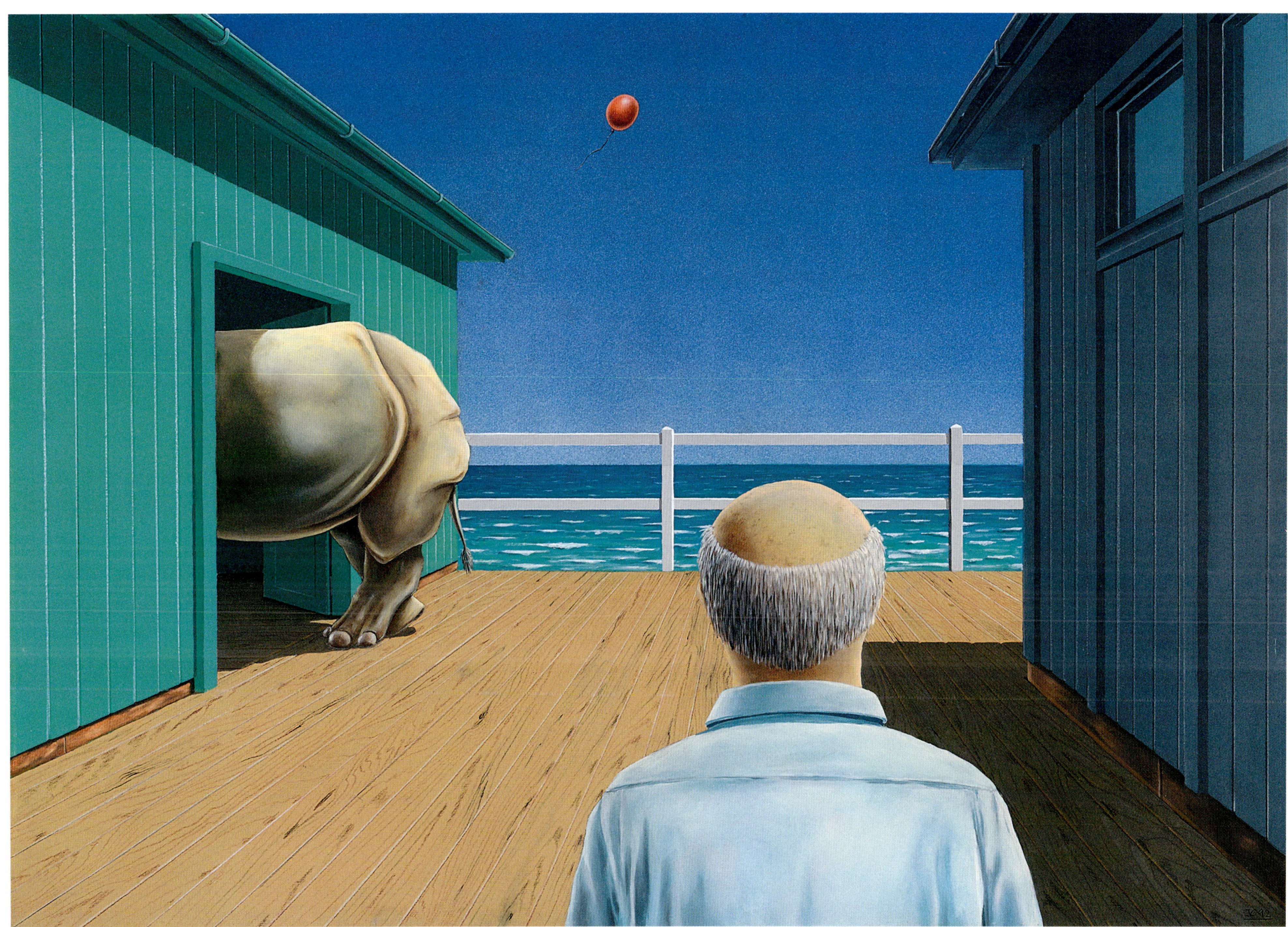

Jacob Samuel McCullurs war ein guter, äußerst beliebter Pfarrer. Sonntags war die Kirche jeweils bis auf den letzten Platz besetzt. Doch nachdem er sein Buch »Es gibt keinen Gott, das ist so sicher wie das Amen in der Kirche« veröffentlichte, blieben die Bänke leer und der Kirchenrat legte ihm nahe, sich doch vorzeitig pensionieren zu lassen, was er dann auch tat. Seither lebt er zurückgezogen und widmet sich ganz seinem geliebten Pianospiel und seinem kleinen Geheimnis.

Jacob Samuel McCullurs was a good, extremely popular pastor. On Sundays the church was always filled to capacity. But after he published his book "There is no God, that is as certain as the amen in the church", the pews remained empty and the church council suggested that he retire early, which he did. Since then, he has lived in seclusion, devoting himself entirely to his beloved piano playing and his little secret.

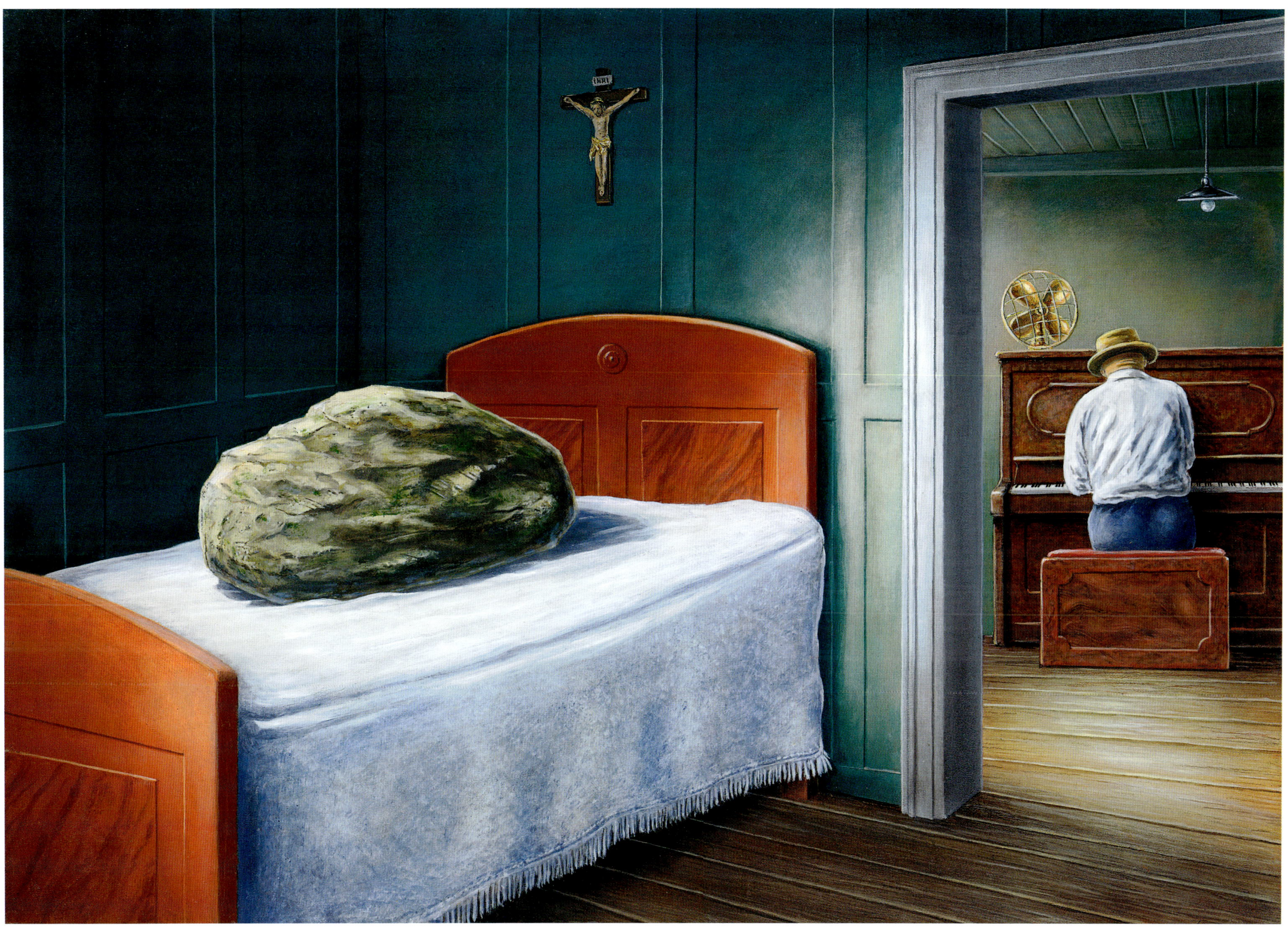

Die unendlich langen und einsamen Tage eines vollkommen überflüssigen Heiligen

The endless and lonely days of a completely superfluous saint

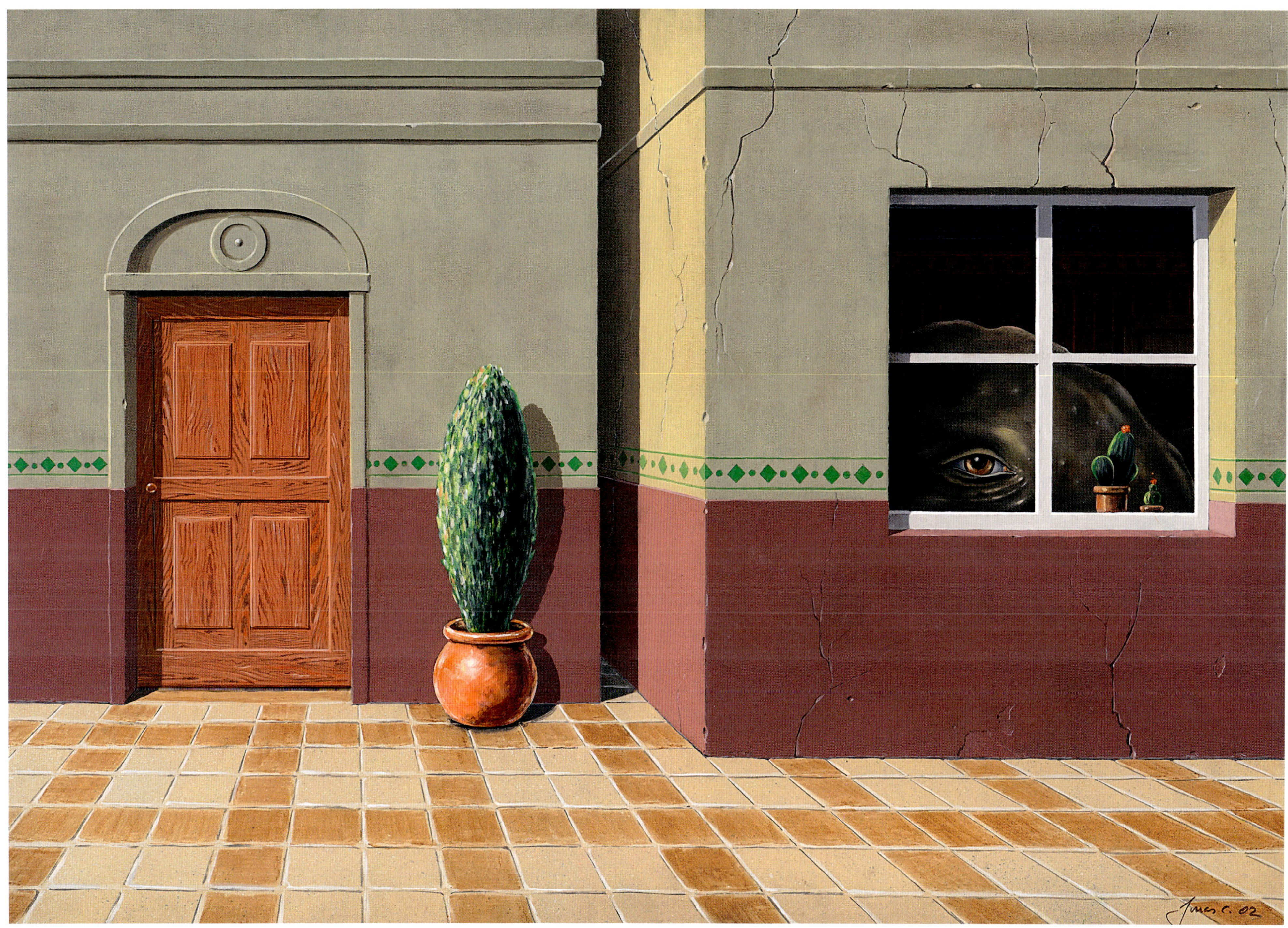

Die Erleuchtung
des 17ten Buddhagurumahtra

The enlightenment
of the 17th Buddhagurumahtra

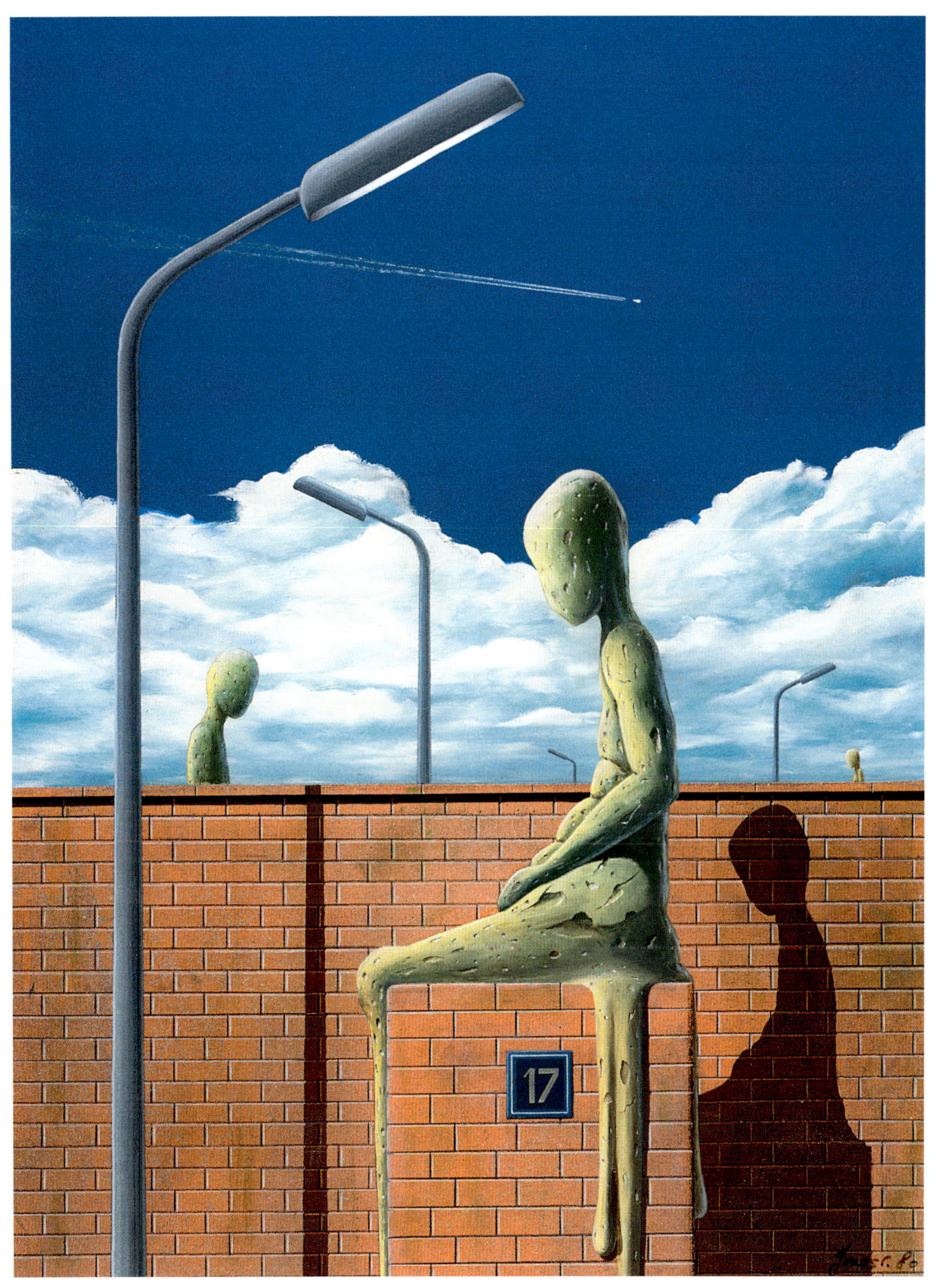

17

Anfänglich war Eberhardt Feigenwinter Jr., leitender Angestellter im Bundesamt für nicht bestellte oder unbefriedigende Schicksale (BAS), sehr skeptisch, aber jetzt ist er mit seiner neuen Assistentin Cäcilie mehr als zufrieden.

Initially, Eberhardt Feigenwinter Jr., a senior employee at the Federal Bureau of Unsettled or Unsatisfactory Fate (FBF), was very skeptical, but now he is more than satisfied with his new assistant Cäcilie.

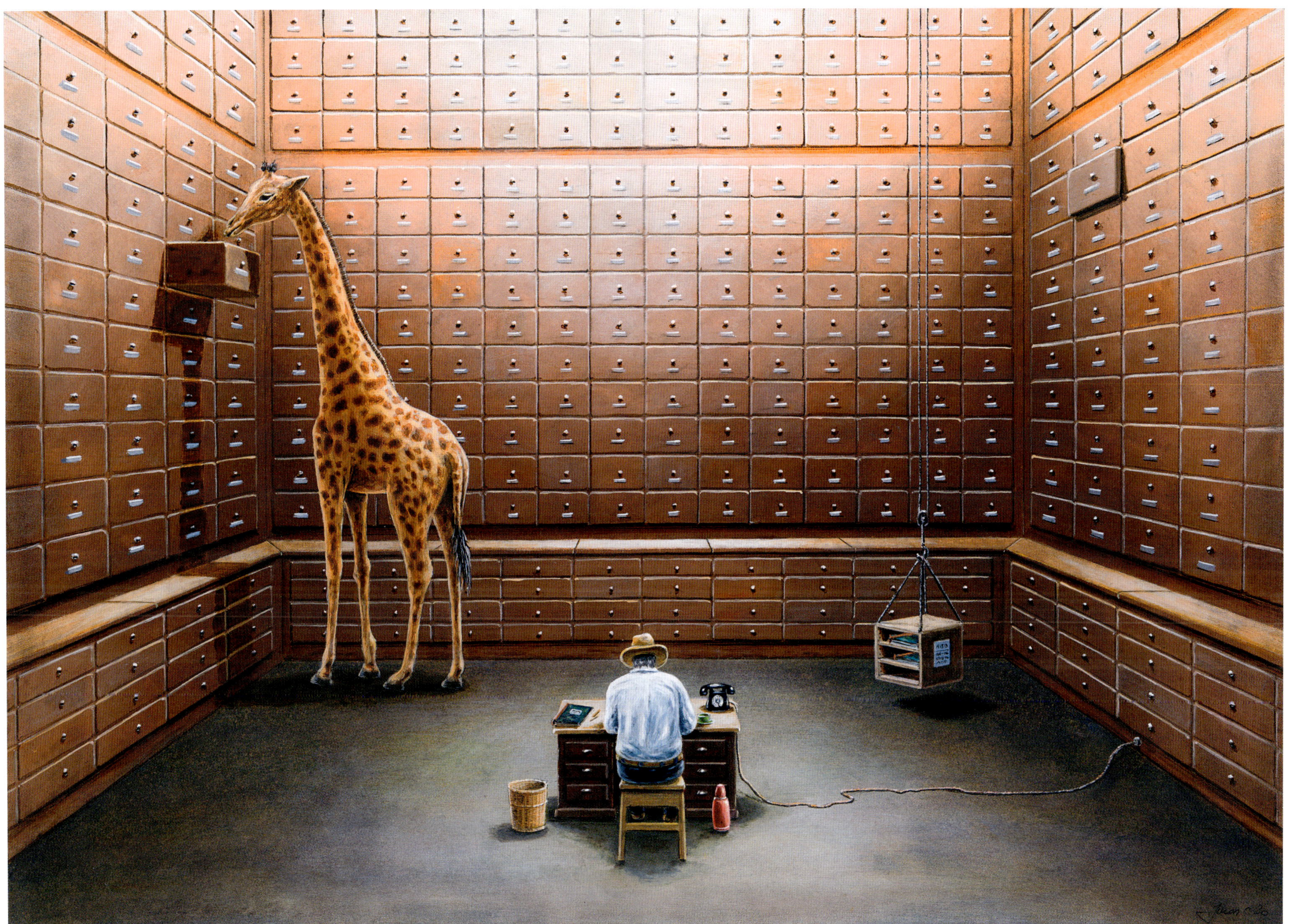

Eine unheimliche Begegnung

An uncanny encounter

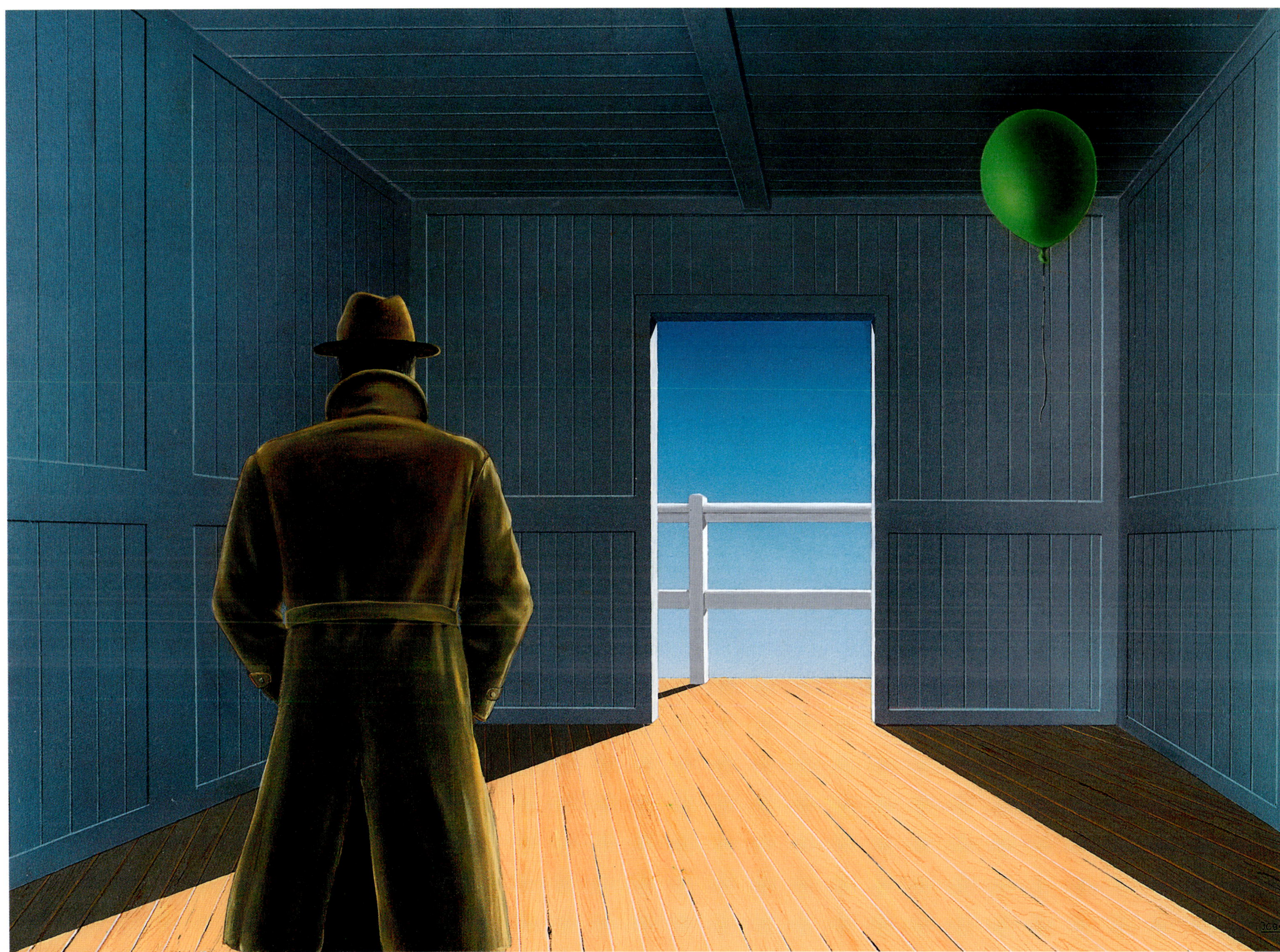

<u>1994</u>

Dieser denkwürdige Freitag begann für Hans-Walter mit einem doch sehr überraschenden und für ihn äußerst verstörenden Besuch …

For Hans-Walter, this memorable Friday began with a very surprising and for him extremely disturbing visit …

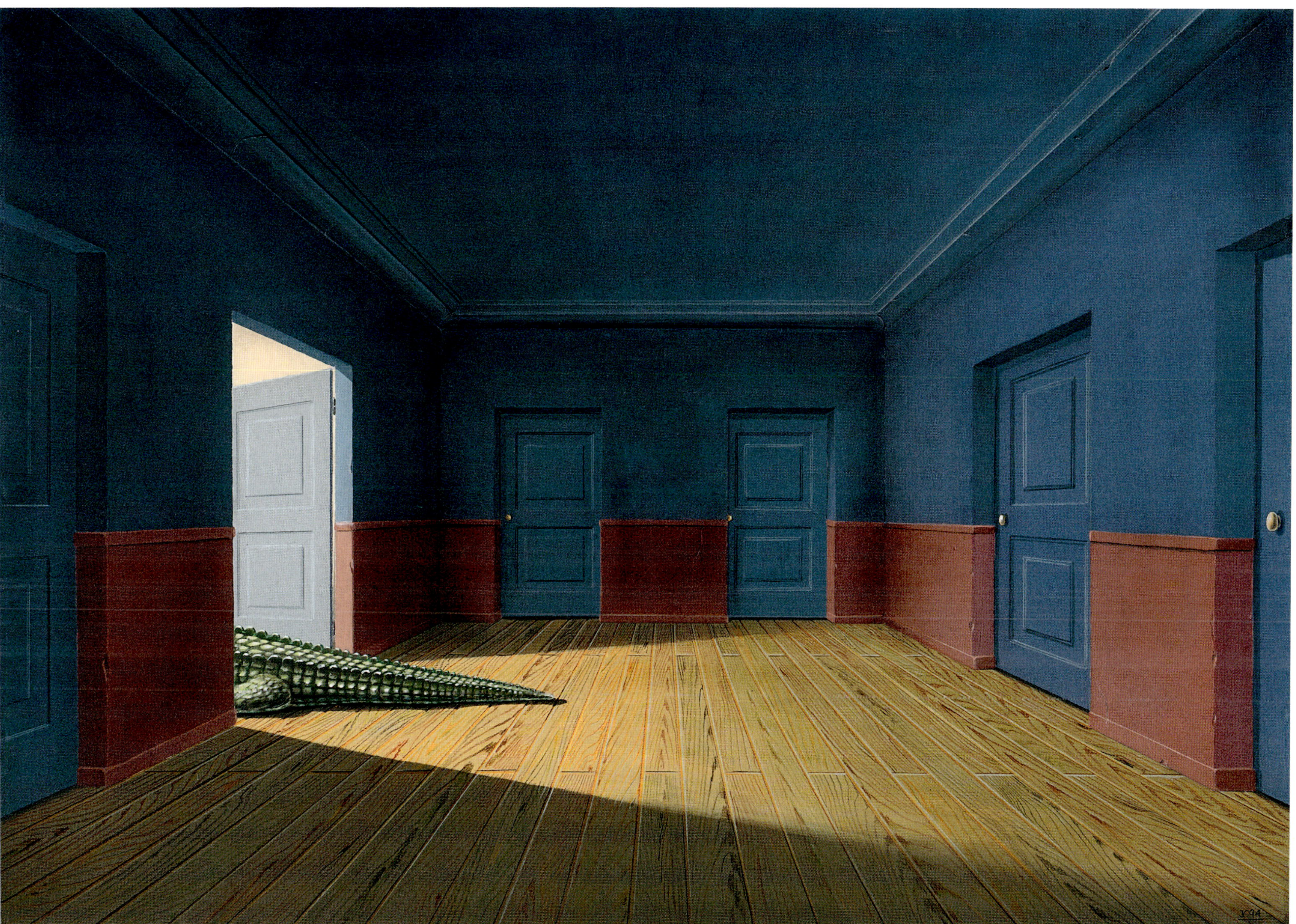

Was für ein herrlicher Albtraum
oder Abendstimmung am schönen
Traubachertalsee

What a wonderful nightmare
or Evening mood at the beautiful
Traubachertal lake

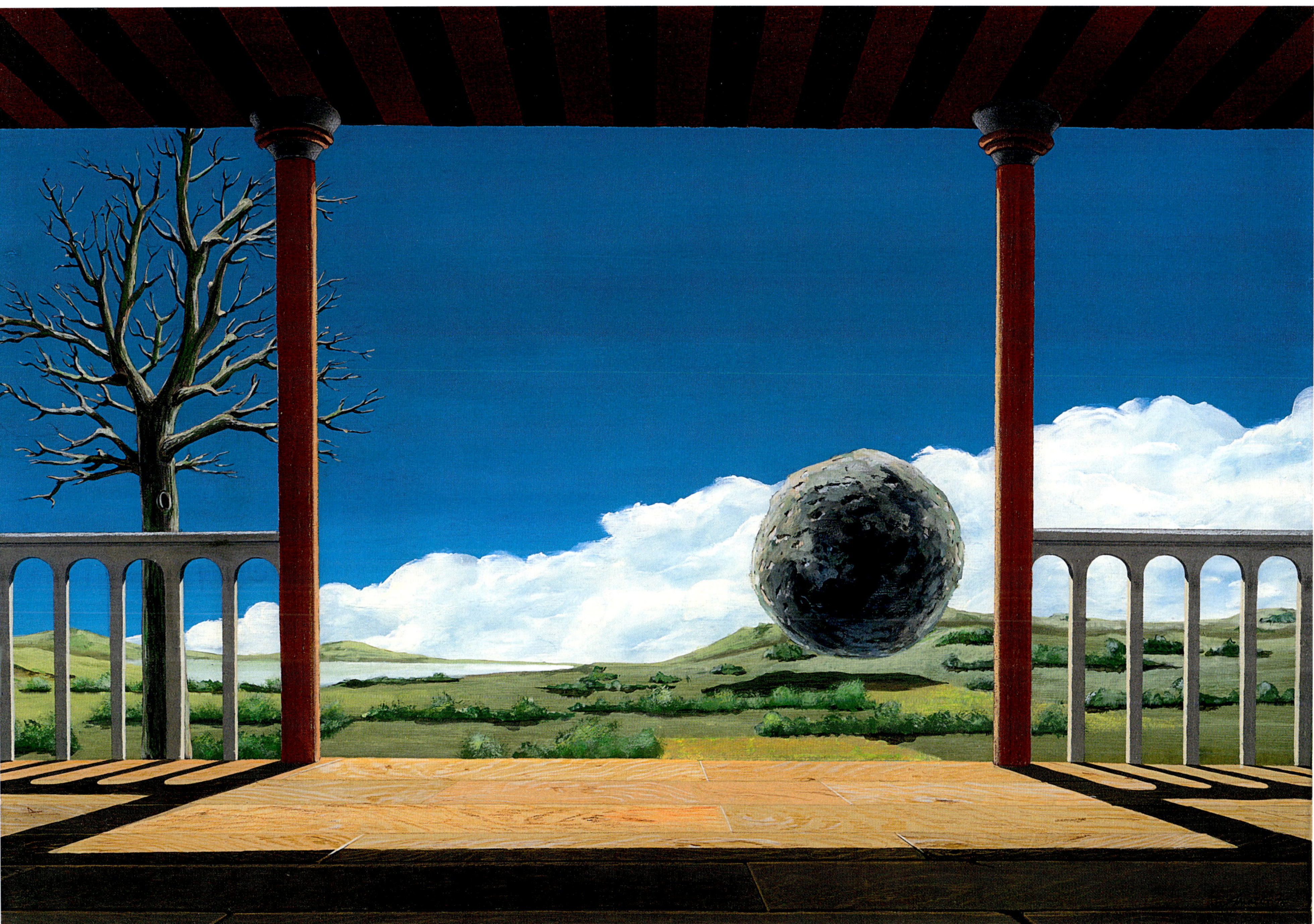

Die pazifische Giraffenschnecke (giraffdae peloris oceanus) legt tausende von Kilometern zurück und überwindet jedes Hindernis, um an ihren ursprünglichen Laichplatz zurückzukehren.

The pacific giraffe snail (giraffdae peloris oceanus) travels thousands of kilometers and overcomes every obstacle to return to its original spawning site.

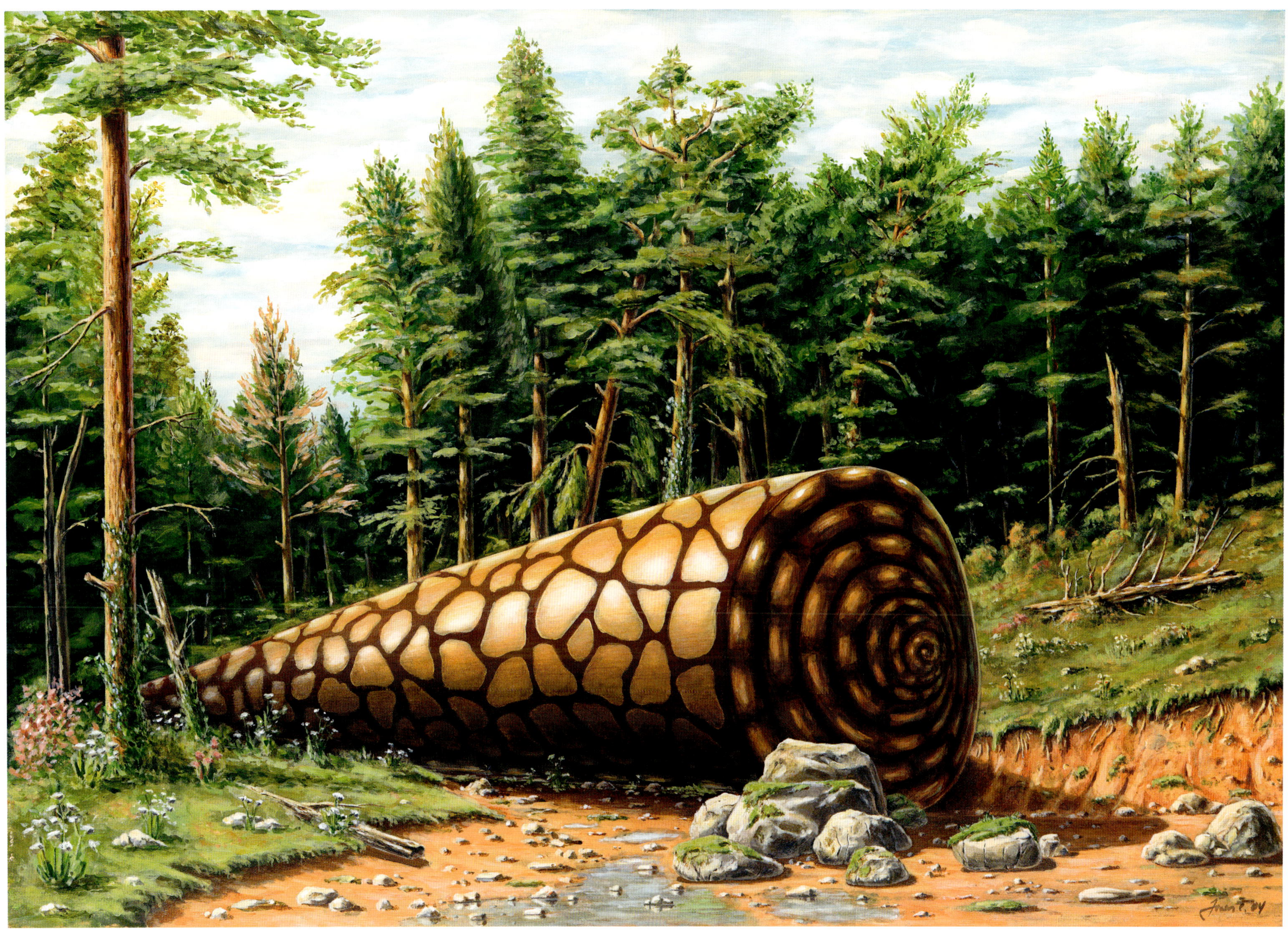

<u>2015</u>

Der Realität zu entfliehen
ist keine Kunst, aber es ist eine Kunst,
sich darin zurechtzufinden

Escaping reality is not an art,
but finding your way around it is

Hommage an Peter Bräuninger, Künstler

Hommage to Peter Bräuninger, artist

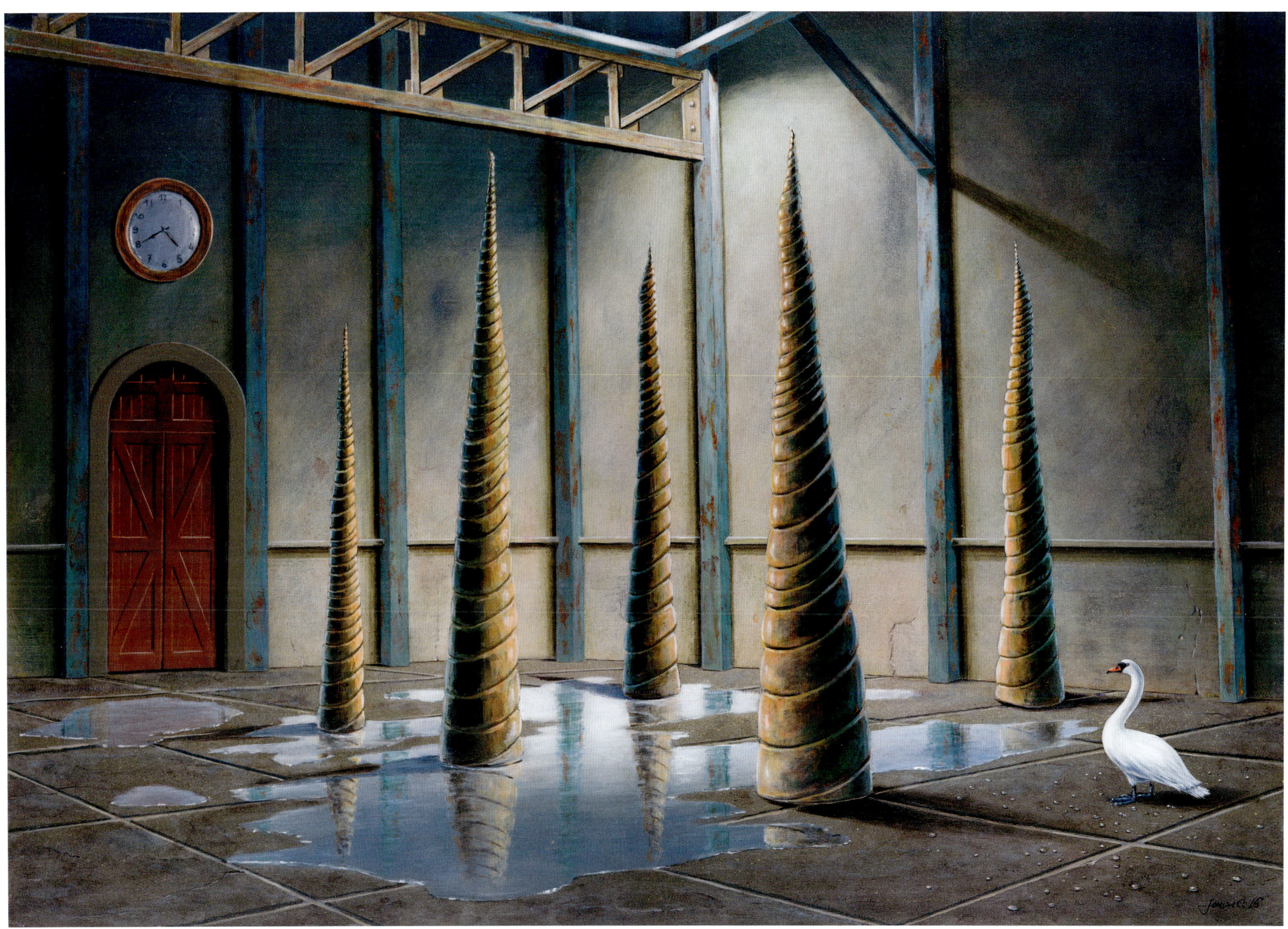

Dr. Dipl. phil. Erhardt Fischbein-Schuler,
Direktor des städtischen Walfisch-Museums
von Obergamsbach und Ehrenpräsident
der Niederbayrischen Vereinigung der Fliegen-
fischer. Seine Dissertation über die unter
Fischen weitverbreitete Seekrankheit gehört
heute zu den Standardwerken der Tiermedizin.

Dr. Dipl. phil. Erhardt Fischbein-Schuler,
director of the municipal whale museum of
Obergamsbach and honorary president of
the Lower Bavarian Association of Fly Fishers.
His dissertation on seasickness, which is
widespread among fish, is now one of the
standard works in veterinary medicine.

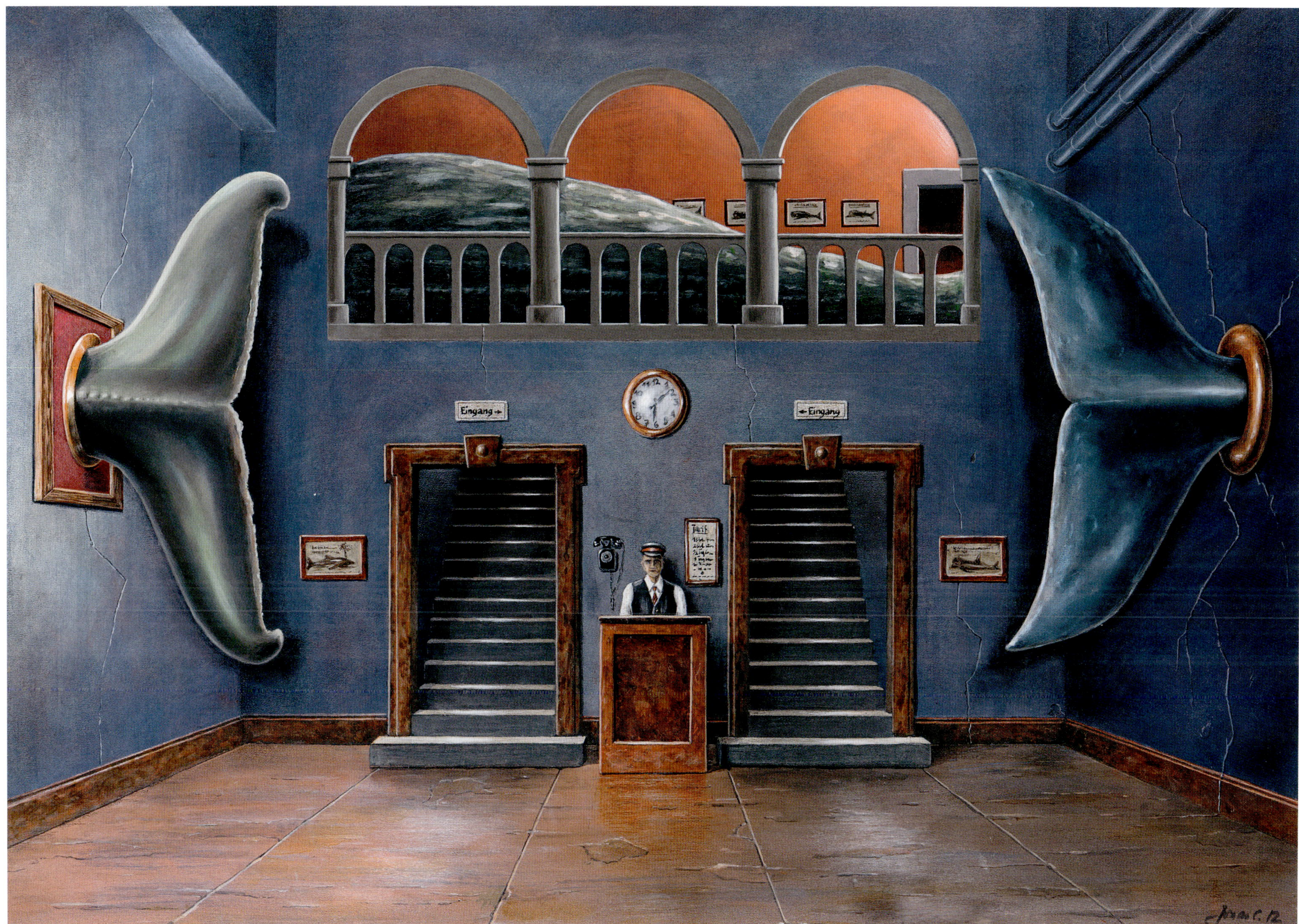

Eingang →
← Eingang
Tarif

Nostalgie der Zukunft

Nostalgia of the future

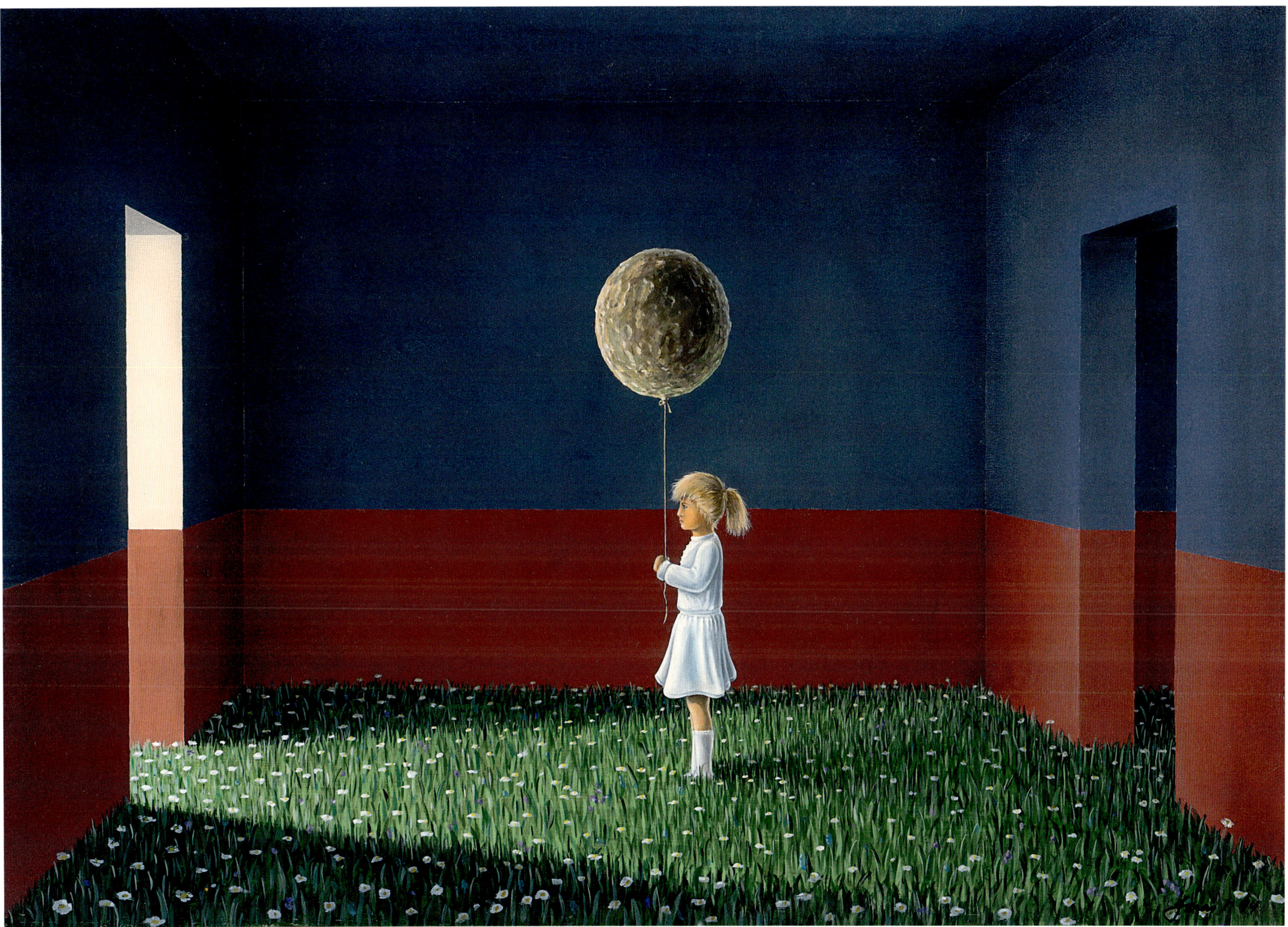

**Das kleine Missgeschick des kleinen Herbert
oder Wenn Träume in Erfüllung gehen**

The little mishap of little Herbert
or When dreams come true

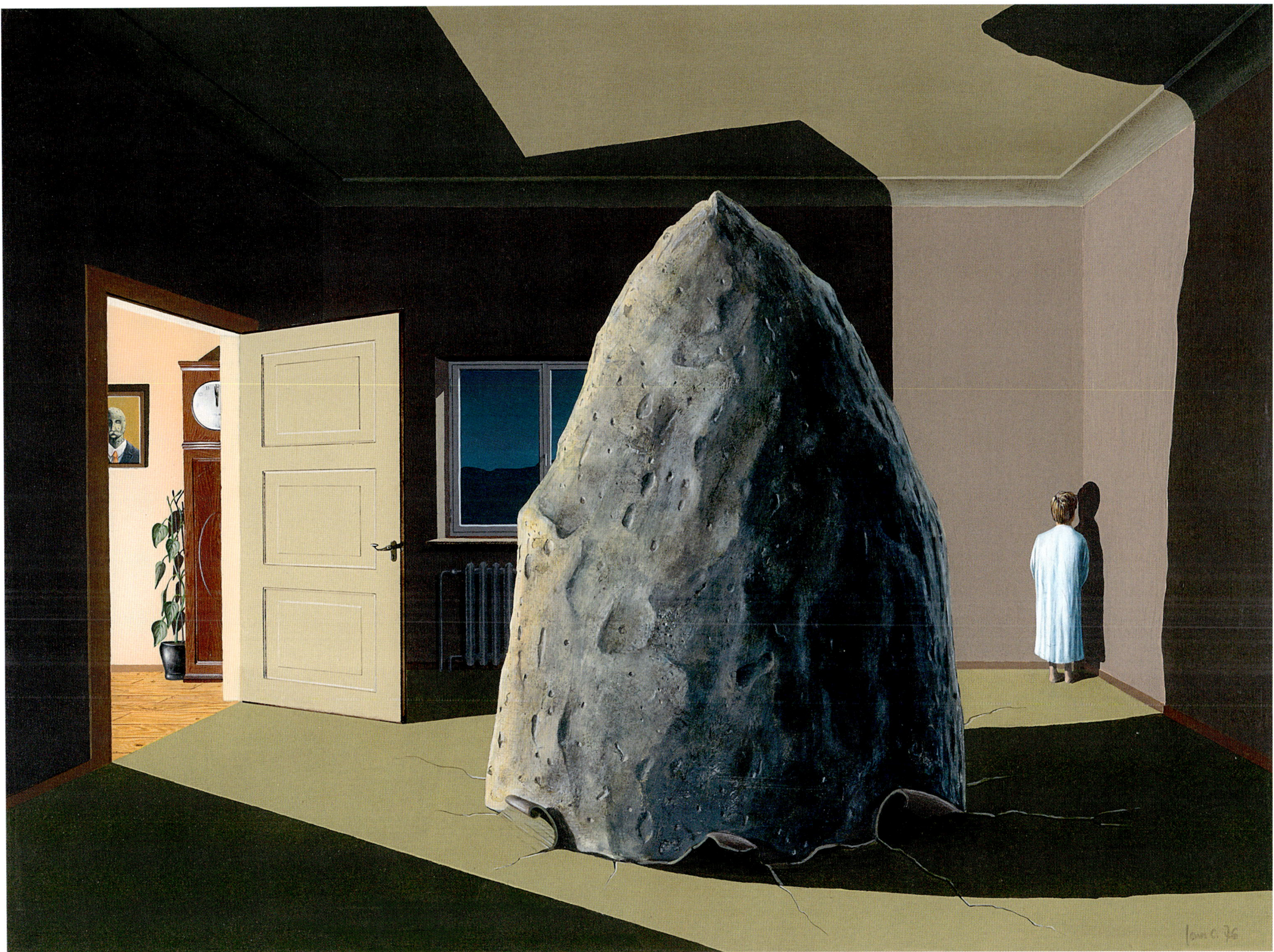

<u>1975</u>

**Die Hartnäckigkeit einer
sehr jungen Wolke**

The stubbornness of
a very young cloud

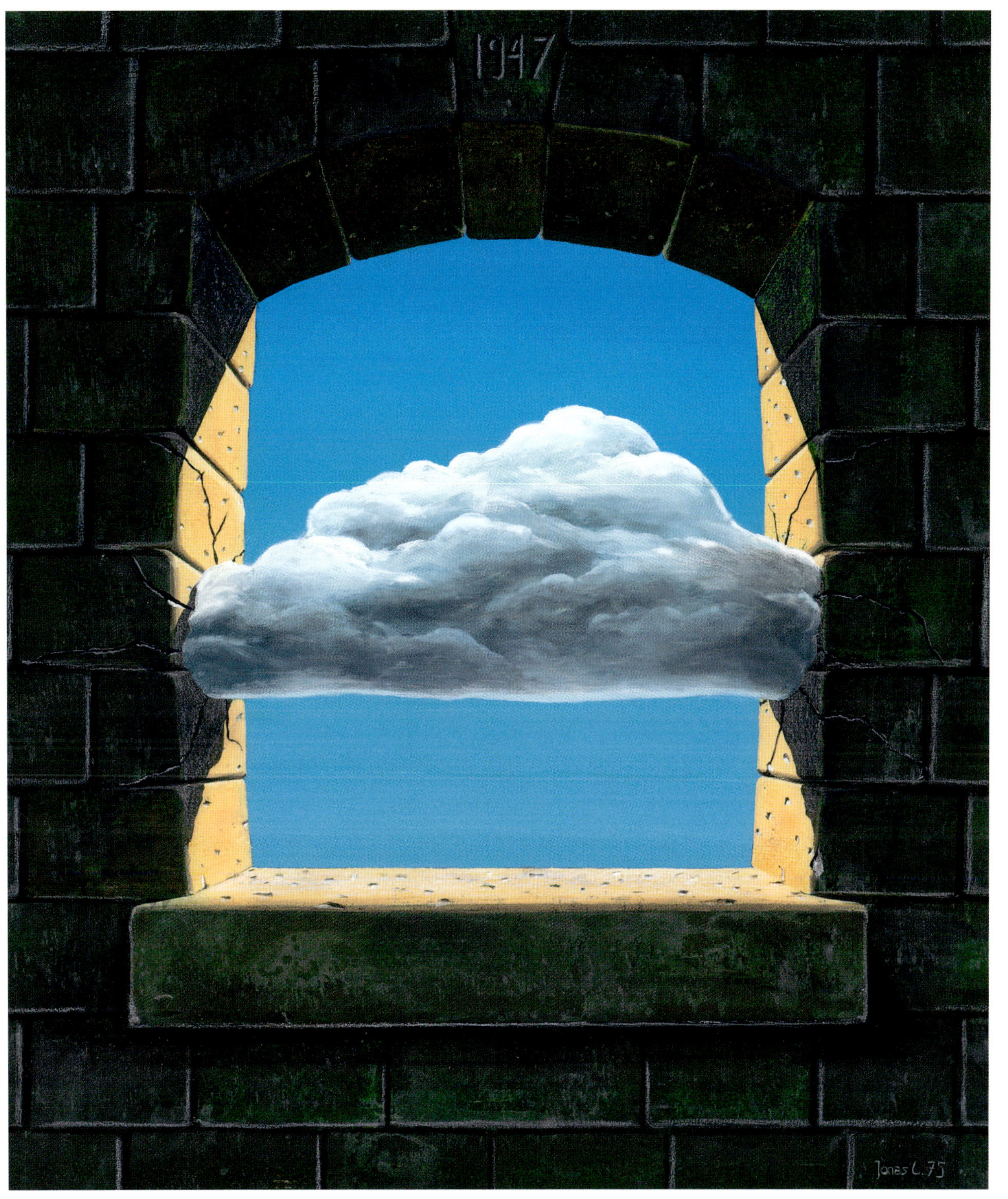

1947
Jones L. 75

Alle haben mal klein angefangen　　　　We all started small

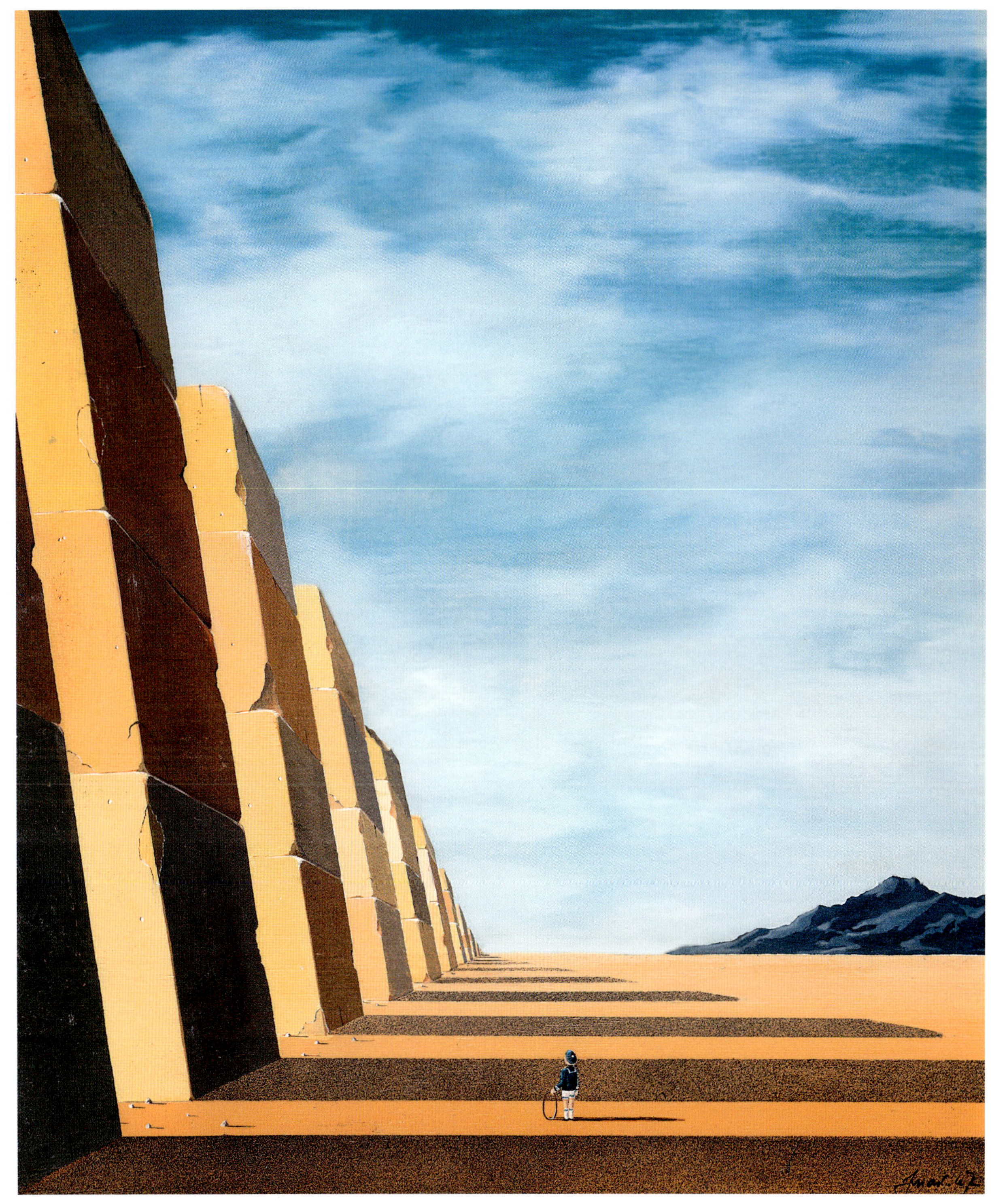

Suche die sieben Unterschiede
und behalte zwei

Find the seven differences
and keep two

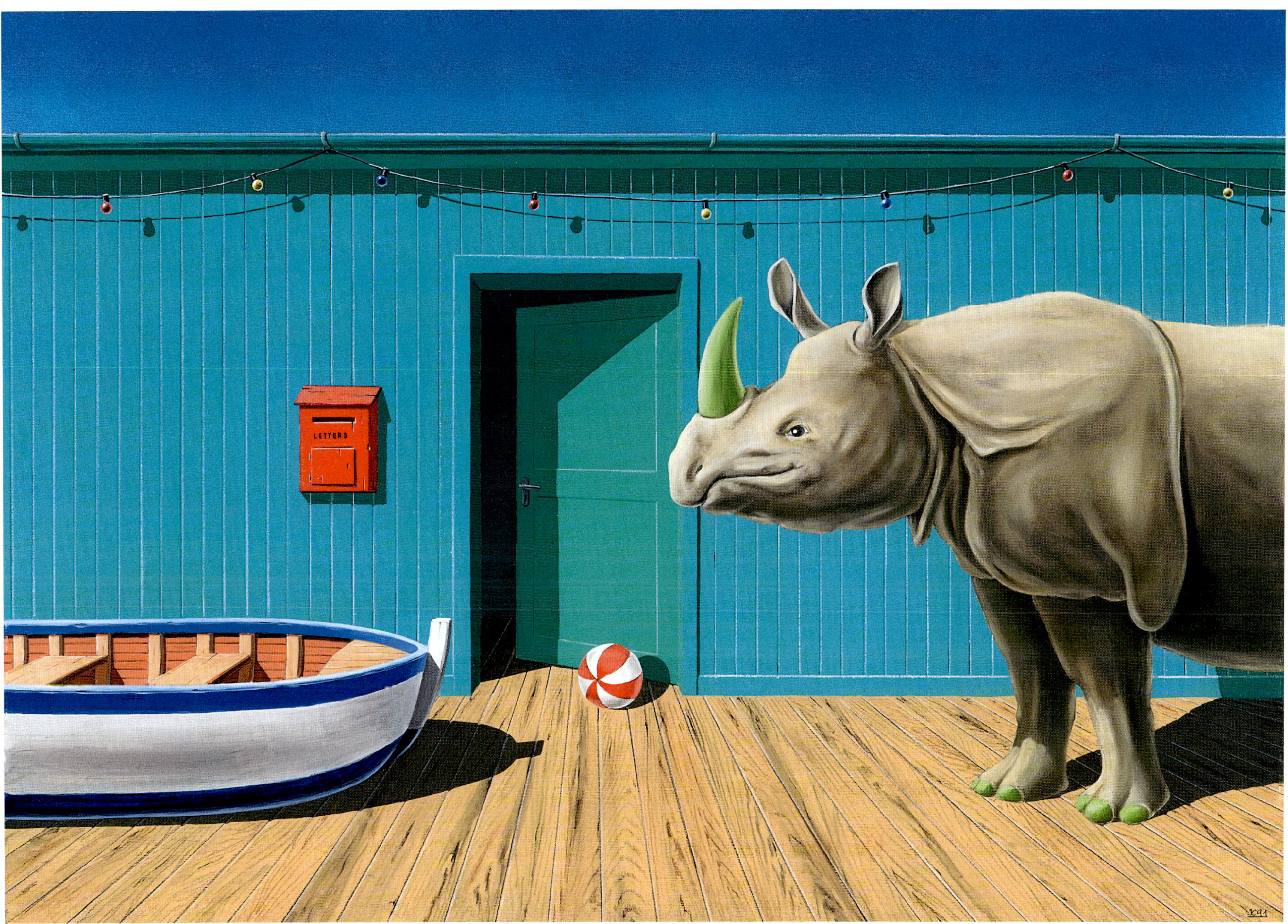
LETTERS

Der Traum der Fische

The dream of the fishes

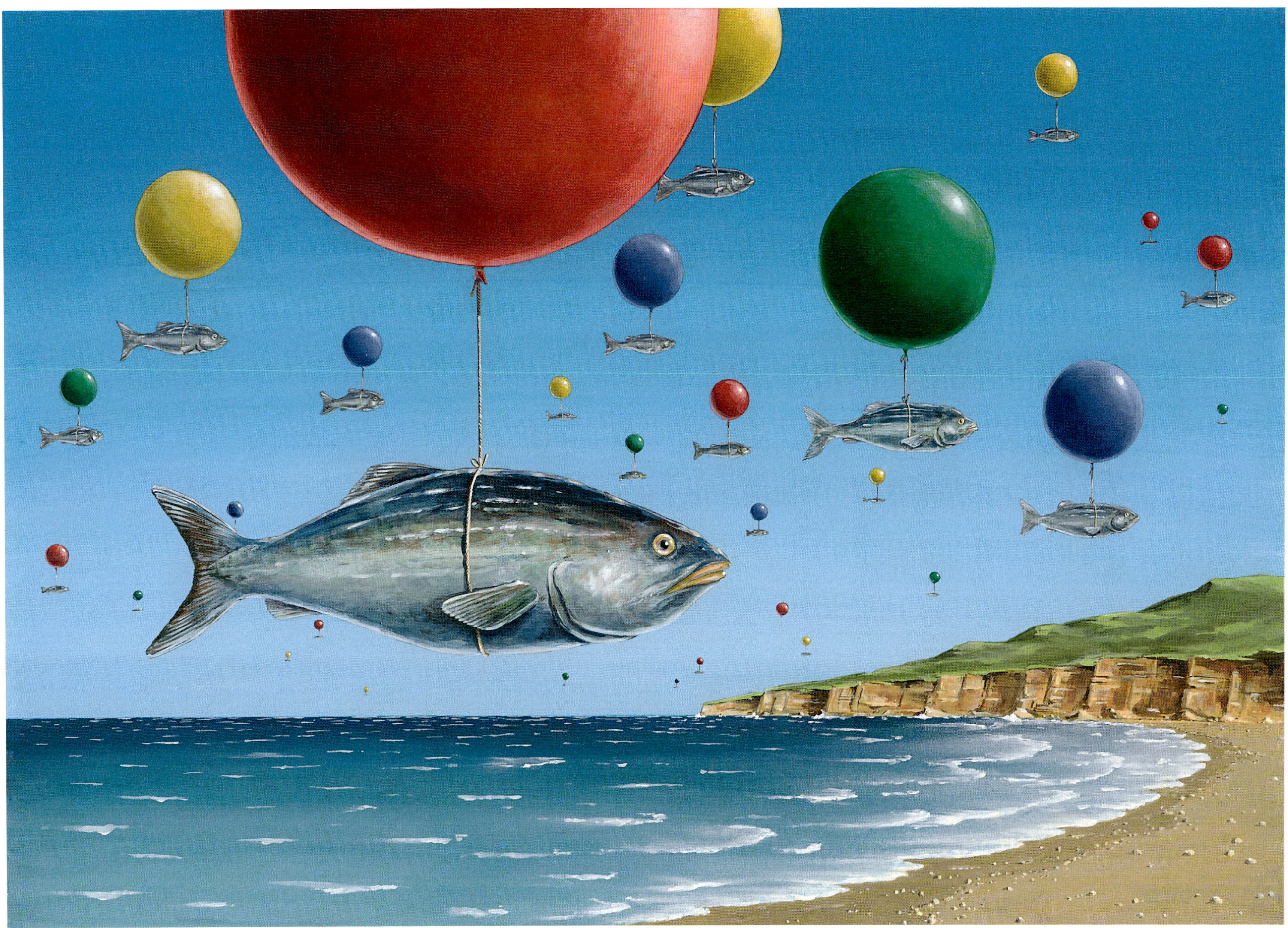

Alexandre Antoine Puiol
(* 1. Juni 1857 in Marseille; † 8. August 1945)
besser bekannt unter seinem Künstlernamen
»Monsieur Antoine«, Zwillingsbruder des
legendären Flatulenzkünstlers Josef Puiol,
hatte die außergewöhnliche Fähigkeit seiner
Violine Töne zu entlocken, welche nicht nur
Glas, sondern auch massives Eisen zum
Bersten bringen konnten. Damit erlangte er
weltweiten Ruhm und feierte große Erfolge
auf allen Varieté-Bühnen der Welt.
So sollte er auch bei der Eröffnung der Welt-
ausstellung 1889 in Paris auftreten, was
ihm aber kurzfristig von den Behörden aus
Sicherheitsgründen verwehrt wurde, da der
Erbauer des Eiffelturmes, Gustave Eiffel,
berechtigte und nachvollziehbare Bedenken
äußerte.

Alexandre Antoine Puiol
(* June 1, 1857 in Marseille; † August 8, 1945)
better known by his stage name "Monsieur
Antoine", twin brother of the legendary
flatulence artist Josef Puiol, had the extraor-
dinary ability to elicit tones from his violin
that could not only cause glass but also solid
iron to burst. With this ability he achieved
worldwide fame and celebrated great suc-
cesses on all vaudeville stages of the world.
He was also supposed to perform at the
opening of the World's Fair of 1889 in Paris,
but the authorities refused to allow him to
perform at short notice for safety reasons, as
the builder of the Eiffel Tower, Gustave Eiffel,
expressed justified and understandable
concerns.

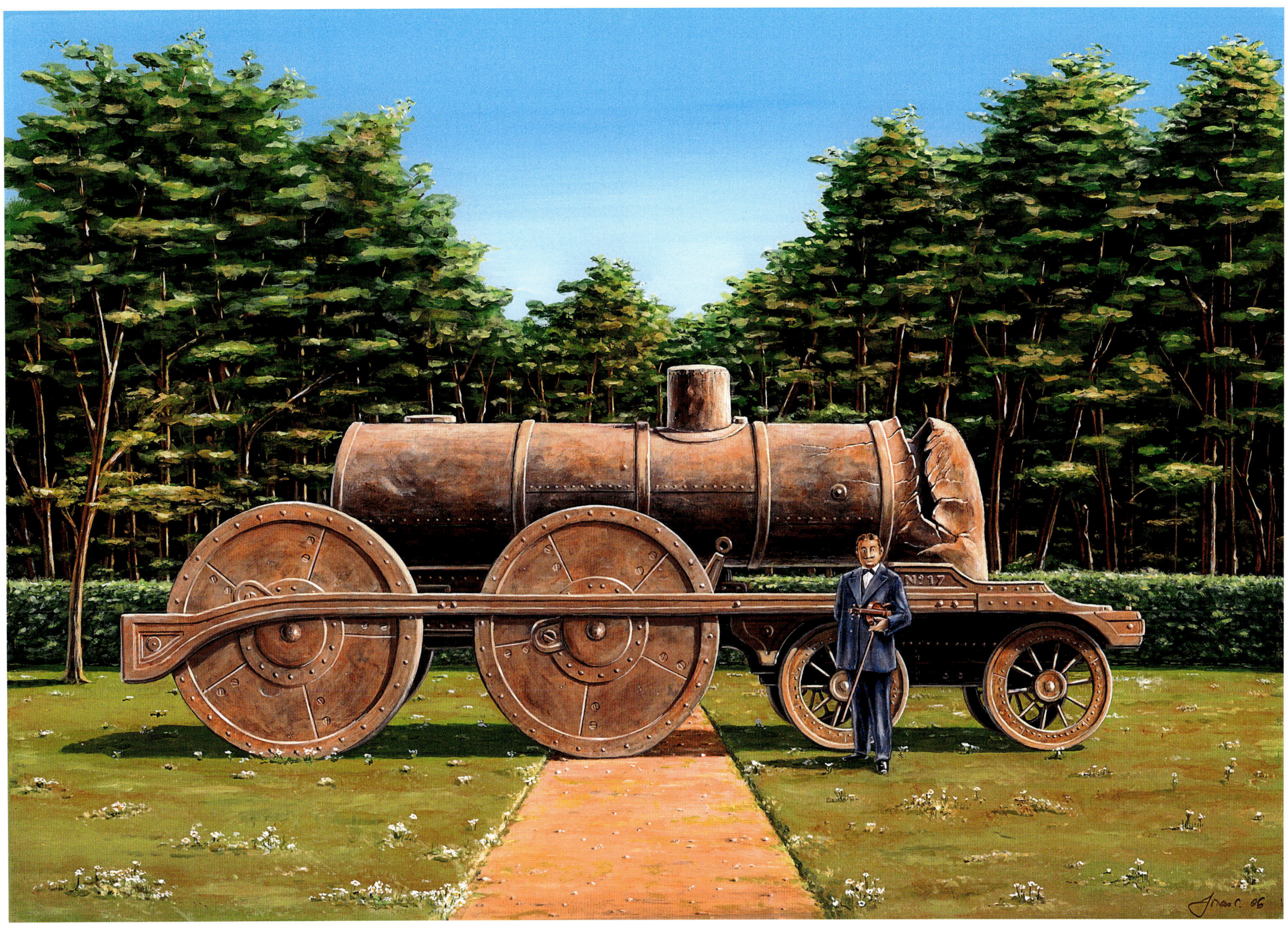

Großraumschnecken werden bis zu 150 Jahre alt und übertreffen bezüglich der Energie-Effizienz die kühnsten Erwartungen

Large-capacity screws can live up to 150 years and exceed the boldest expectations in terms of energy efficiency

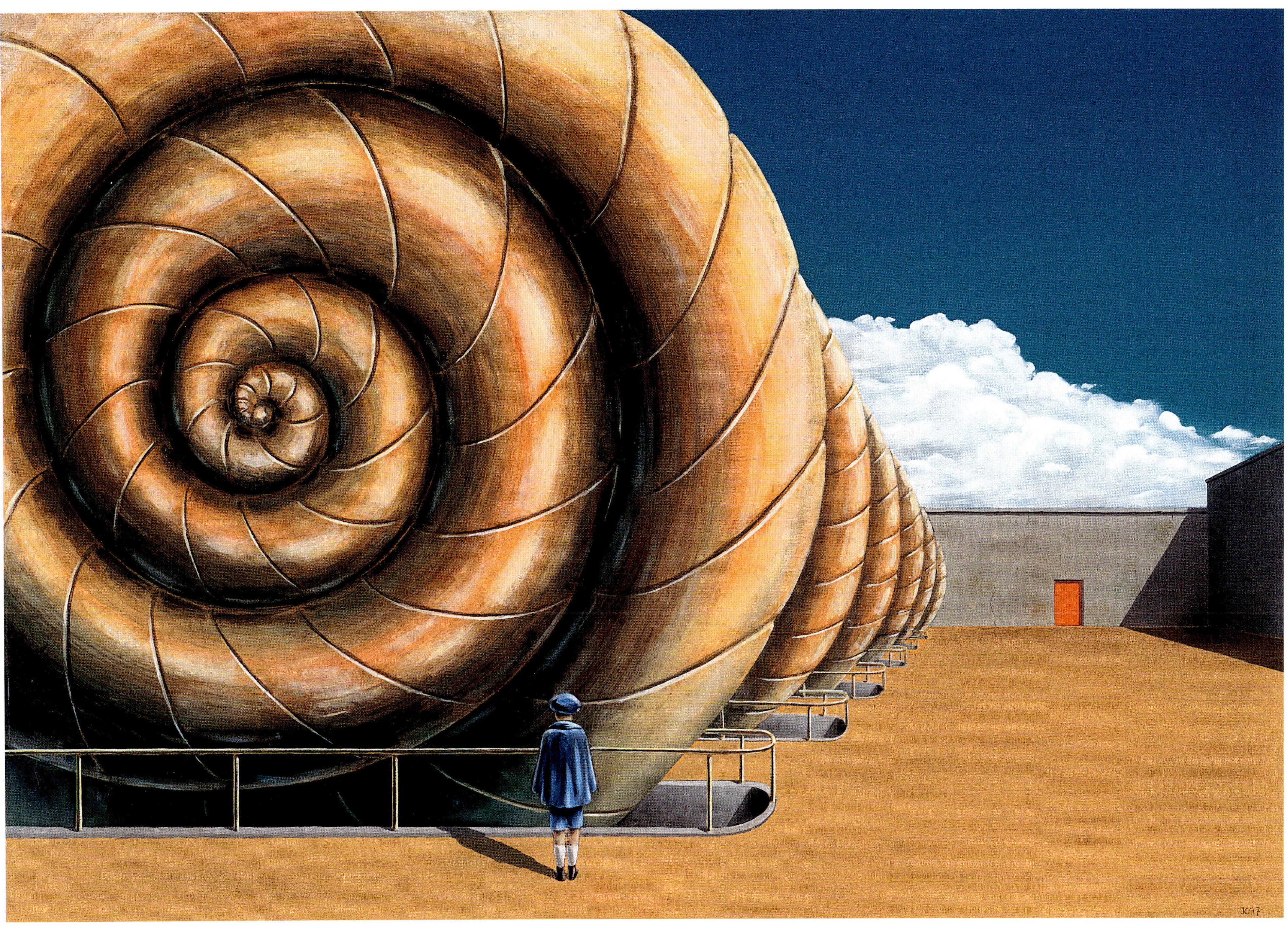

Helmut C. Schlitzowitz ist vielleicht der beste und der wohl berühmteste Wolken-Porträtfotograf aller Zeiten. Seine großformatigen, atemberaubenden Bilder sind heute in allen großen Museen der Welt zu sehen und erzielen bei Auktionen Spitzenpreise.
Seit dem 13. August 2022 gilt er allerdings als verschollen und wird vermisst. Von offizieller Seite heißt es, er sei von einem Blitz getroffen worden, ins Meer gestürzt und ertrunken.
Aber vielleicht hat er sich ganz einfach – wie seine Freunde glauben – mit der schönen Claudia, seiner Lieblingswolke, welche er immer und immer wieder fotografierte, heimlich davongemacht.
Aber das ist nur ein Gerücht.

Helmut C. Schlitzowitz is perhaps the best and probably the most famous cloud portrait photographer of all times. His large-format, breathtaking images can now be seen in all major museums of the world and fetch top prices at auctions. Since August 13, 2022 however, he has been missing. Officials say he was struck by lightning, fell into the sea and drowned. But perhaps – as his friends believe – he simply made off secretly with the beautiful Claudia, his favorite cloud, whom he photographed over and over again. But that is just a rumor.

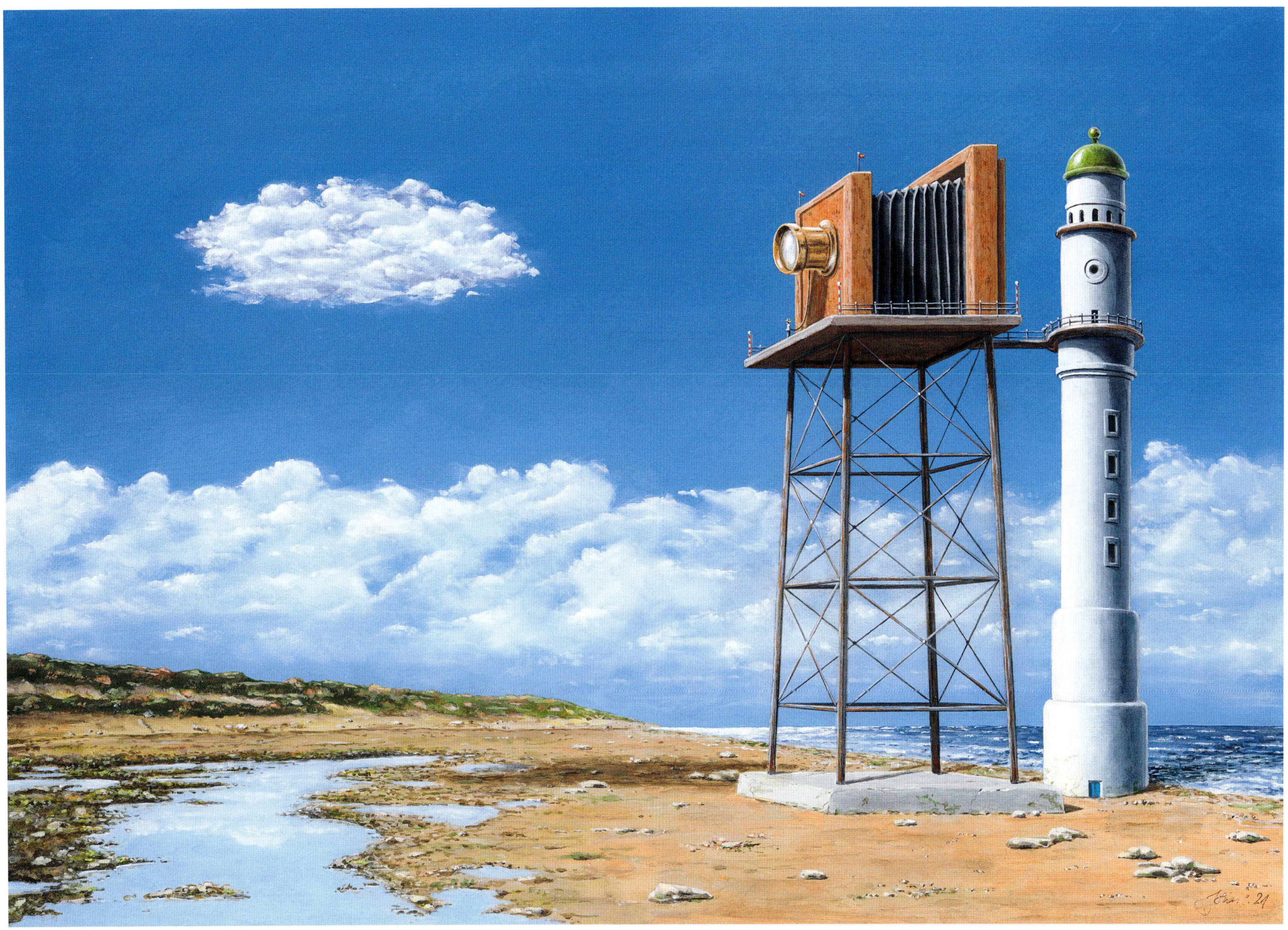

Herr und Frau Müller-Schumann gönnen sich auch dieses Jahr wieder eine mehrmonatige luxuriöse Kreuzfahrt auf dem oberen Chalbermattsee.

Mr. and Mrs. Müller-Schumann treat themselves again this year to a several months luxurious cruise on the upper Chalbermatt lake.

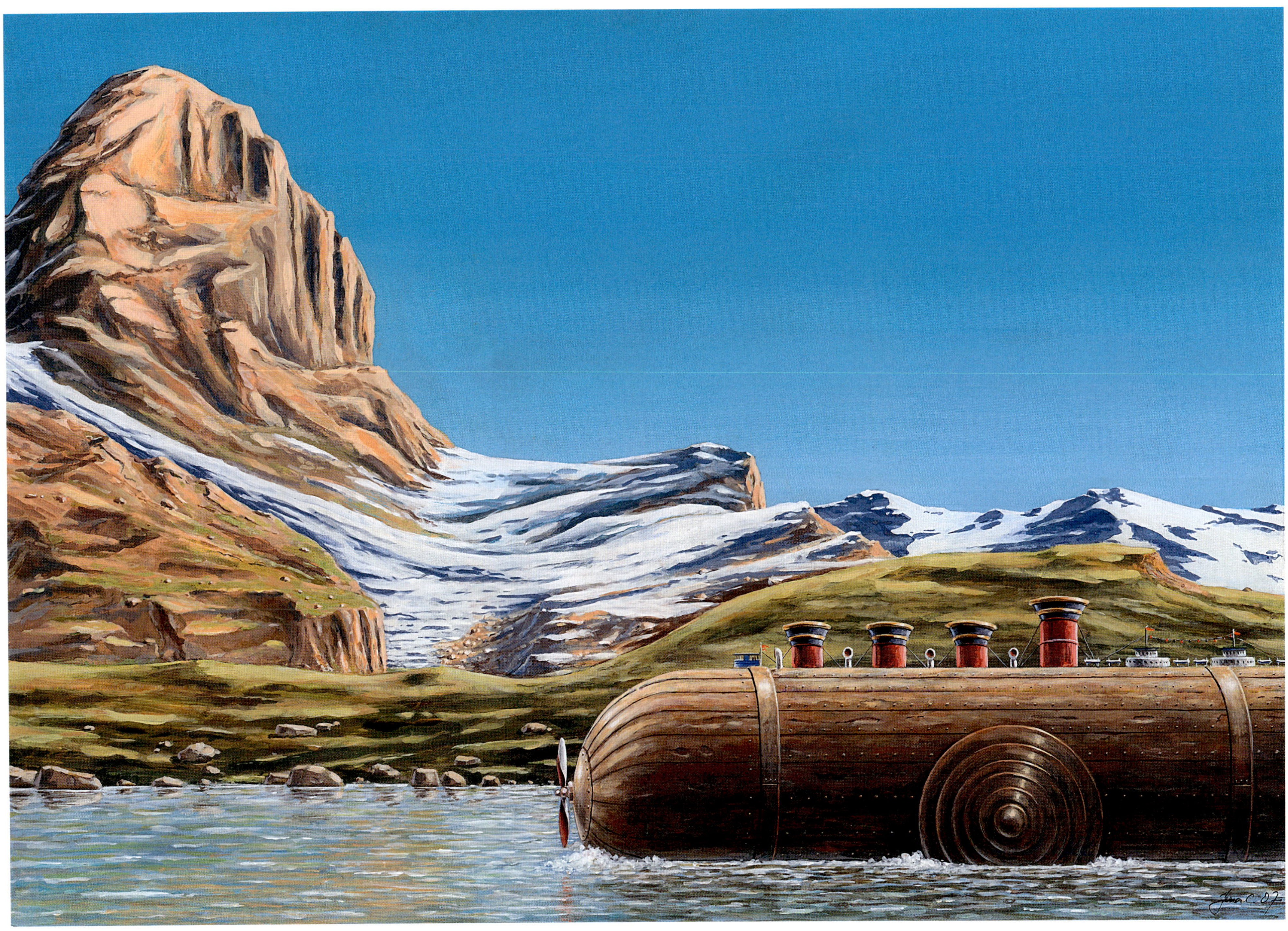

Als Esmeralda Leticia Marques ihre Hoch-
wand-Telefonie 1956 patentieren ließ, konnte
sie nicht ahnen, dass ein paar Jahre später
mit der Einführung des WWP (World Wide
Phone) ihre Erfindung zum Einsatz kommen
und einen nie gesehenen Siegeszug um
die ganze Welt antreten würde. Heute ist
HWC (High Wall Communication) aus dem
Alltag des modernen Menschen nicht mehr
wegzudenken und hat die Welt wesentlich
näher zusammengerückt.

When Esmeralda Leticia Marques patented
her high-wall telephony in 1956, she could not
have imagined that a few years later, with the
introduction of the WWP (World Wide Phone)
her invention would be used and would start
an unprecedented triumphal procession
around the globe. Today, HWC (High Wall
Communication) has become an integral part
of modern life and has brought the world
much closer together.

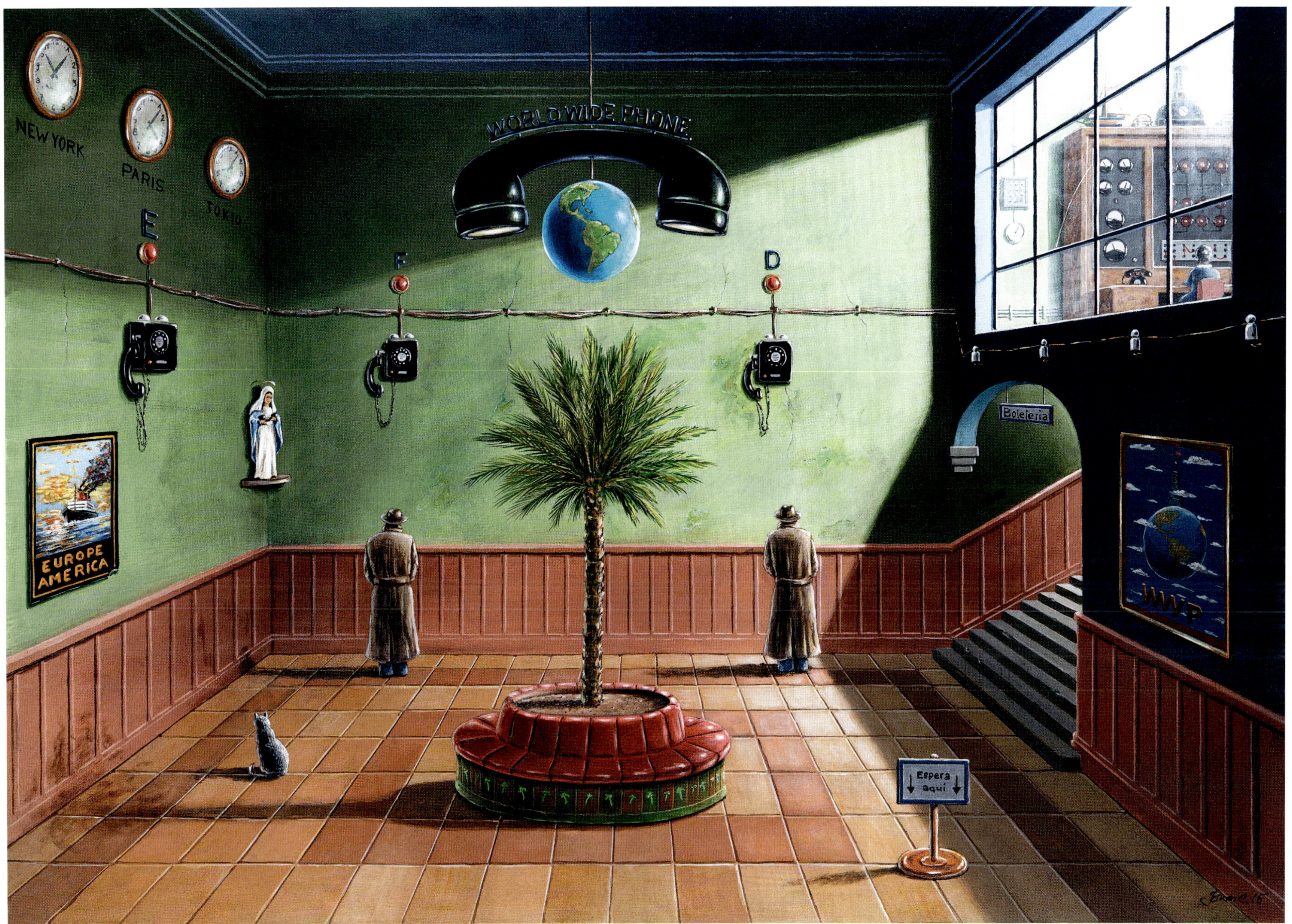

NEW YORK
PARIS
TOKIO
WORLD WIDE PHONE.
E
F
D
EUROPE
AMERICA
Boletería
WWP
Espera
aqui

Blues for a rolling stone

Blues for a rolling stone

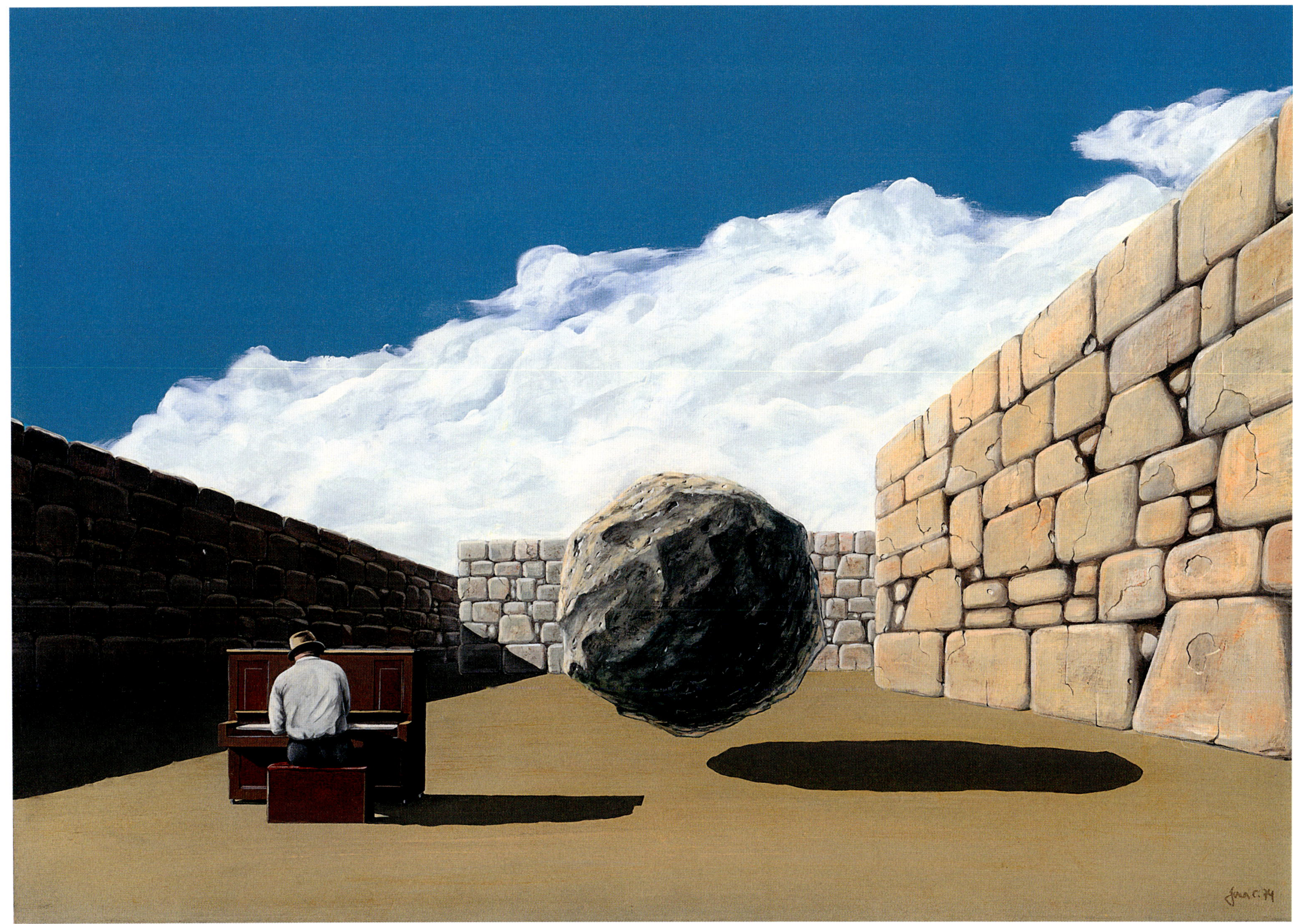

Die Seele eines ausgewachsenen, geschlechts-
reifen Nilpferdes wiegt durchschnittlich 38 g
und ist damit erstaunlicherweise nur unwesent-
lich schwerer als die menschliche Seele
(zwischen 8 und 35 g), wie der renommierte
amerikanische Arzt Duncan MacDougall
(1866–1920) nach unzähligen wissenschaftlichen Experimenten 1902 nachweisen konnte.
(New York Times & American Medicine,
März 1907.)

The soul of an adult, sexually mature
hippopotamus weighs an average of 38 g
and is thus surprisingly only marginally
heavier than the human soul (between 8
and 35 g), as the renowned American physician Duncan MacDougall (1866–1920)
could prove after innumerable, scientific
experiments 1902. (New York Times &
American Medicine, March 1907.)

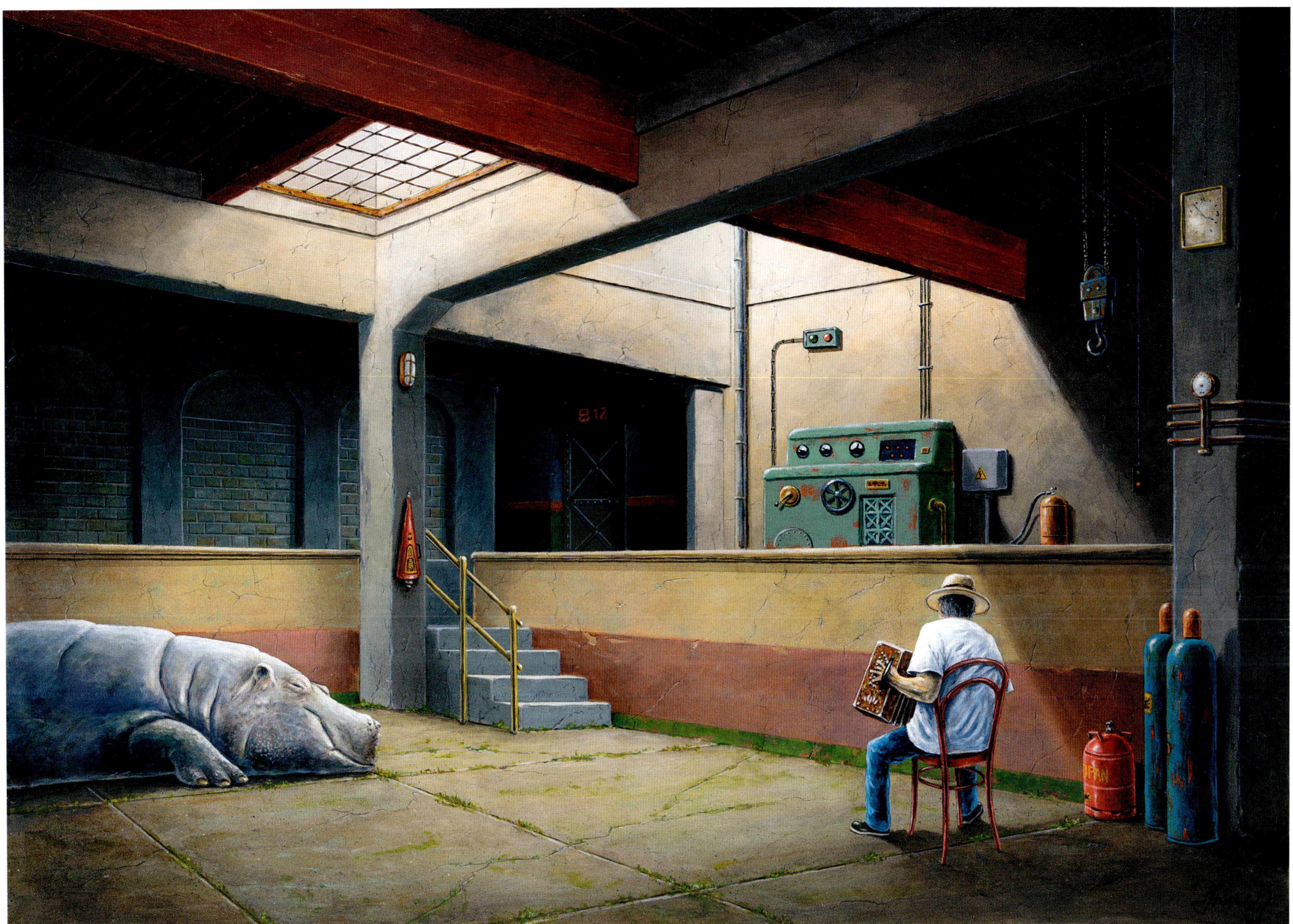

In Gedanken blättert Karl-Heinz immer wieder in seinem Buch »Mein aufregendes und bewegtes Leben«, welches er als 8-Jähriger schreiben wollte, aber nie geschrieben hat.

In his thoughts, Karl-Heinz keeps leafing through his book "My exciting and eventful life", which he wanted to write as an 8-year-old but never did.

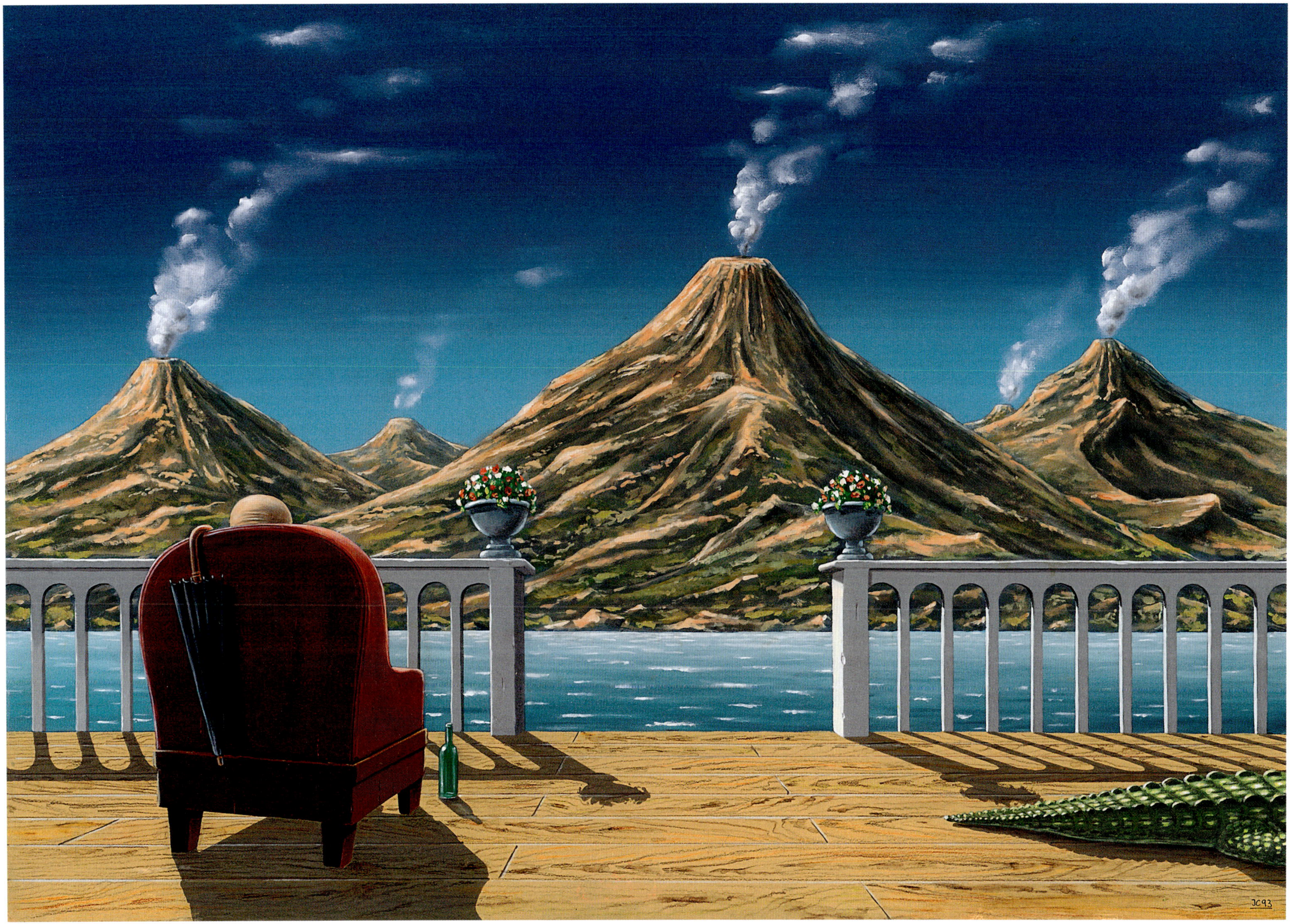

Die weltweit einmalige Altersresidenz
für betagte und pensionierte Leuchttürme
in Porto dei Fari (Italien)

The worldwide unique retirement
residence for aged and retired lighthouses
in Porto dei Fari (Italy)

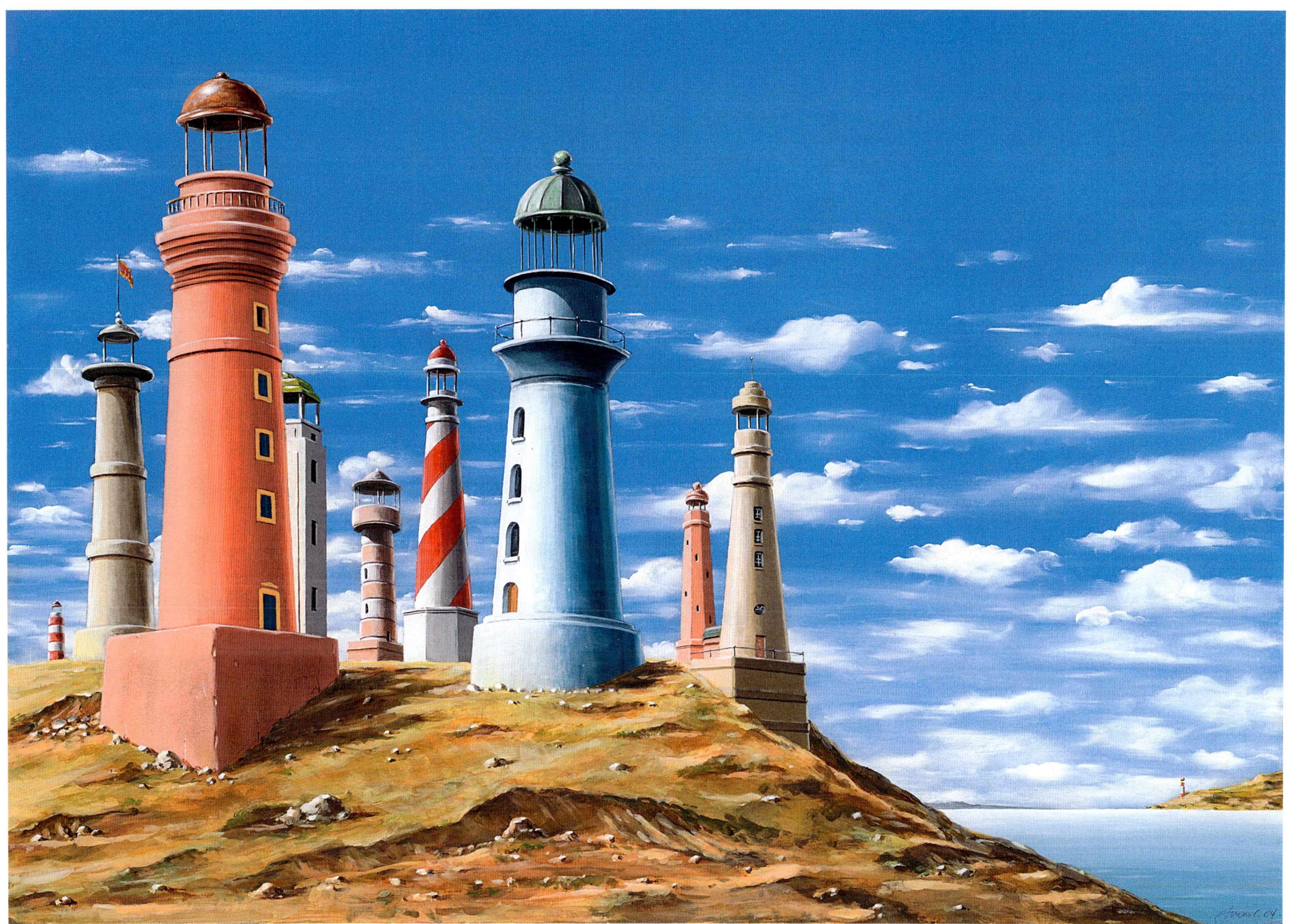

Die berührende Geschichte von Waldemar
dem Vogel, der nicht schwindelfrei war

The touching story of Waldemar the bird
who was not free from giddiness

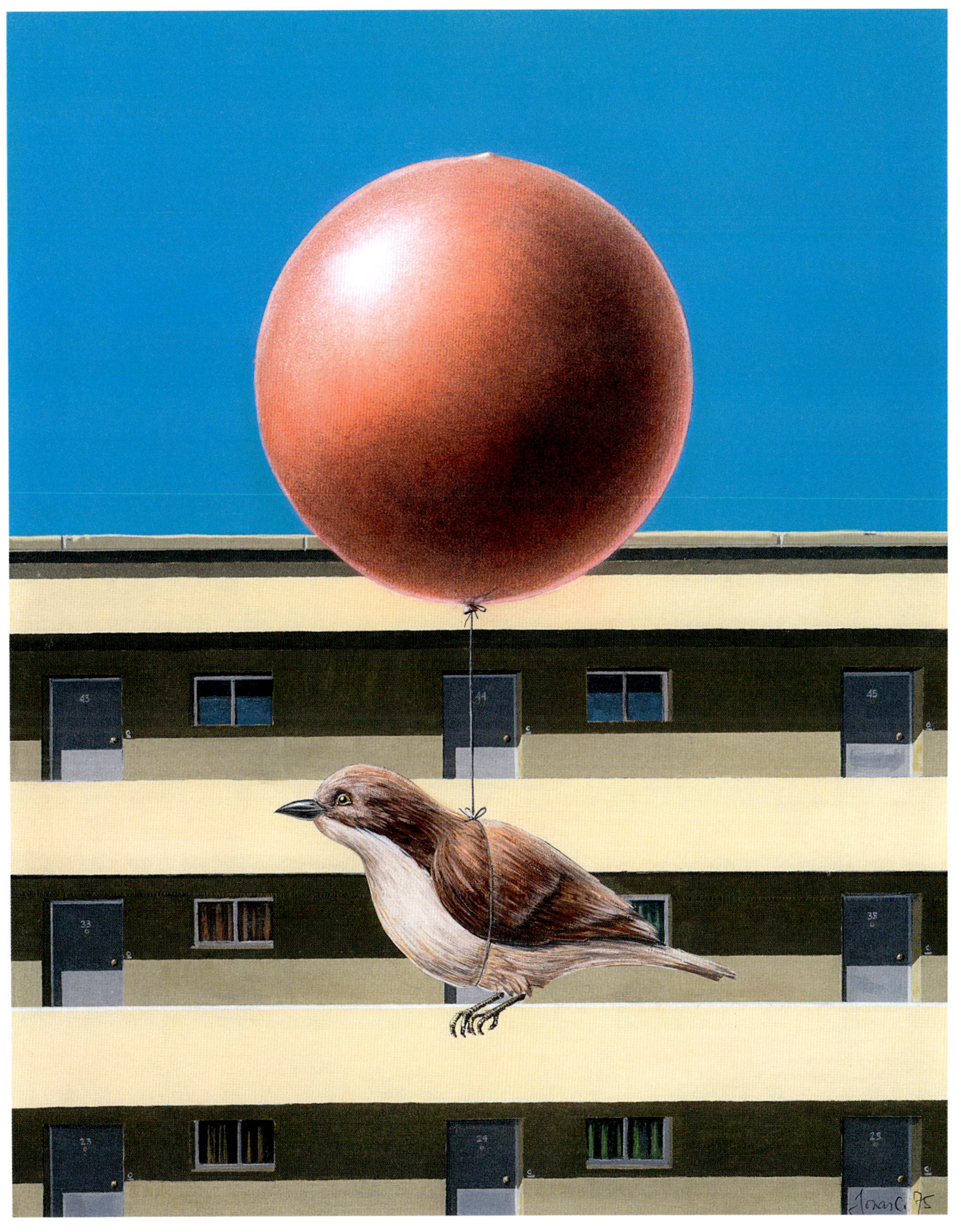

Herr Heim mit Friedrich

Heim, Serge-Hubertus, * 14.6.22 in Straßburg,
unehelicher Sohn des Lacroix-Forbet,
Fabius, studierte angewandte biometrische
Psychologie und Kunstgeschichte in Paris
und Frankfurt, 1951–1959 Dozent an der Univ-
ersität Lausheim, Herausgeber des renom-
mierten Kunstmagazins »Kitsch & Schrott«,
versch. Publikationen, u.a.: »Die geschichtliche
Entwicklung des Scharlatanismus in der Kunst
seit 1968 bis heute«.

Mr. Heim with Friedrich

Heim, Serge-Hubertus, * 6.14.22 in Strasbourg,
illegitimate son of Lacroix-Forbet, Fabius,
studied applied biometric psychology and art
history in Paris and Frankfurt, 1951–1959
lecturer at the University of Lausheim, editor
of the renowned art magazine "Kitsch & Trash",
various Publications, among others:
"The Historical Development of Charlatanism
in Art in art since 1968 until today".

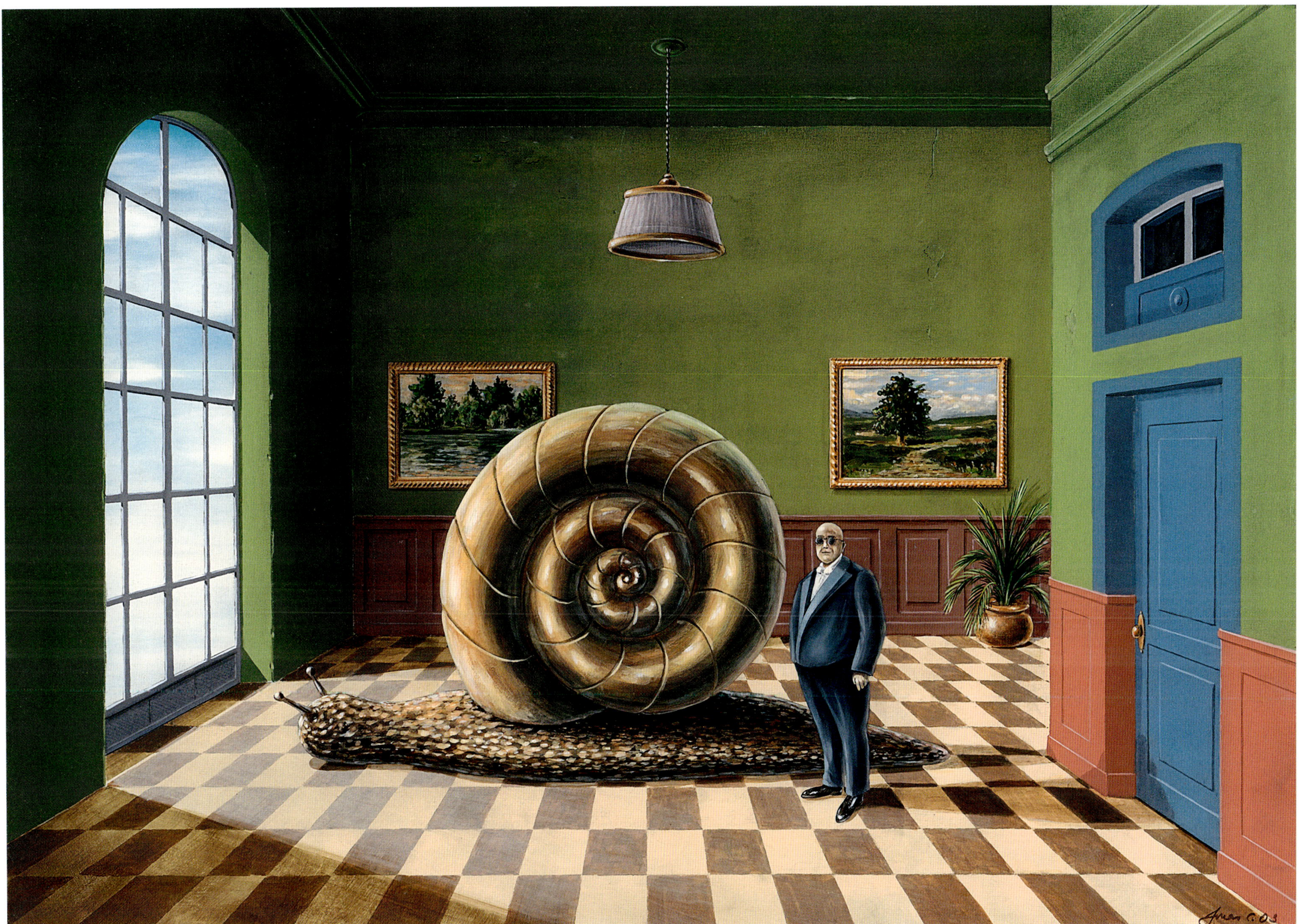

Alois Gürtelbaum, Rotweintrinker
und Kunstsammler

Alois Gürtelbaum, red wine drinker
and art collector

Bild-Zitate/picture quotes:
Garance, Franz Anatol Wyss, Peter Bräuninger,
Alex Sadkowsky, Timmermahn, Hugo Schumacher,
Urs Huber Uri, Kurt Fahrner, Friedrich Kuhn,
Robert Haefeli und Roman Signer's Koffer/bag.

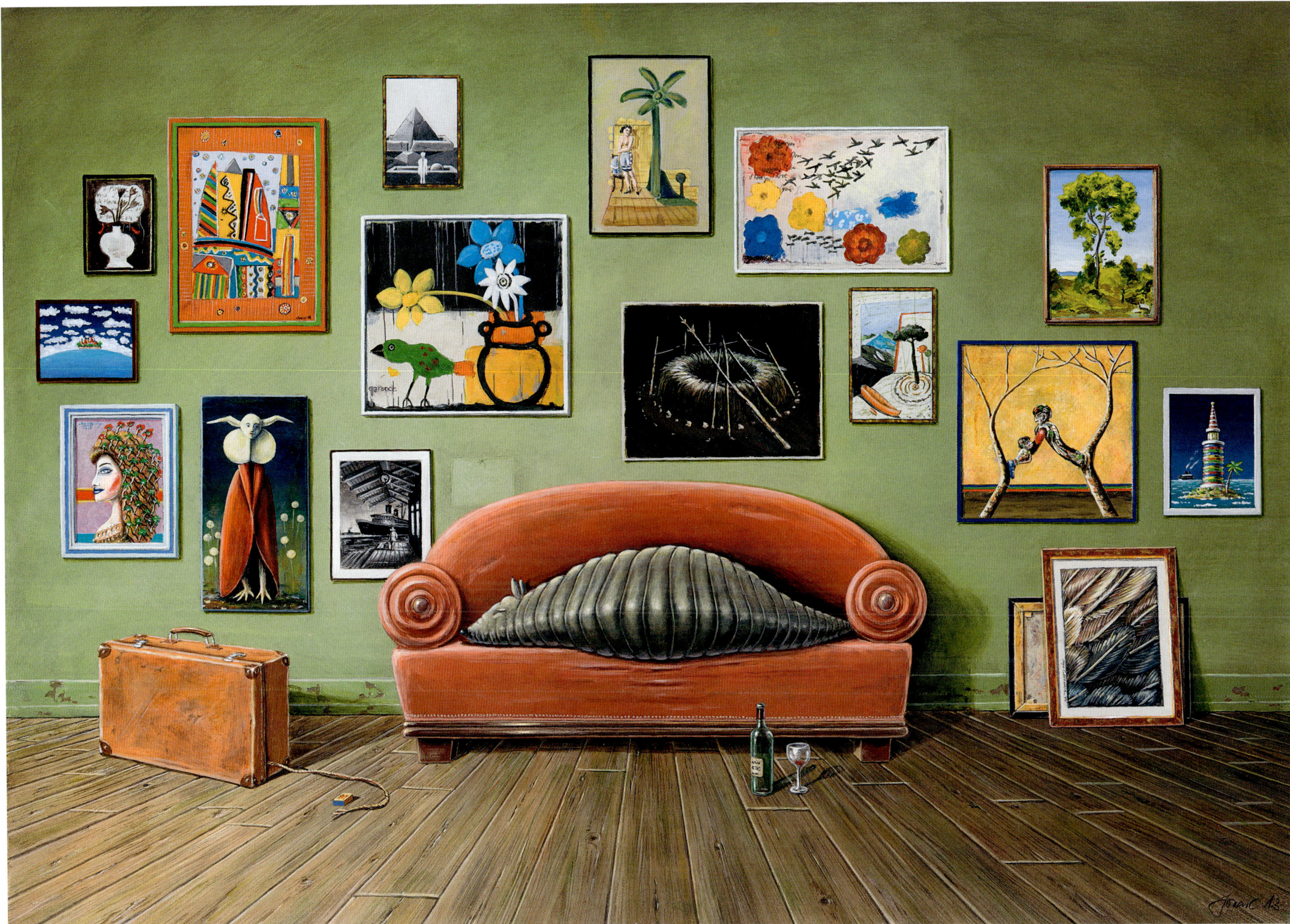

<u>Glossar</u>

Das tragische Leben des »Elephant Man« Joseph Carey Merrick
(1862 bis 1890) wurde 1980 von David Lynch nach wahren Begeben-
heiten mit einer Star-Besetzung verfilmt.

Bei den Zitaten von Sigmund Freud und Albert Einstein handelt es
sich um Original-Zitate.

Den Varieté-Künstler »Monsieur Antoine« hat es nie gegeben, aber
seinen angeblichen Zwillingsbruder, den Flatulenzkünstler Josef Puiol
(1857 bis 1945), welcher mit seiner »Kunst« internationale Erfolge
feierte (»Flatulenzkünstler« ist ein sog. Kunstfurzer).

Sowohl die New York Times als auch American Medicine veröffentlich-
ten 1907 einen Bericht, wonach der amerikanische Arzt Duncan
MacDougall (1866 bis 1920) angeblich nach vielen Experimenten
nachweisen konnte, dass die menschliche Seele durchschnittlich 21g
wiege. Nicht erwiesen ist allerdings, dass er das Gewicht der Seele
eines Nilpferdes bestimmt hat.

Im Bild »Alois Gürtelbaum, Rotweintrinker und Kunstsammler« habe
ich Bilder von Künstlern, mit welchen ich seit Jahren befreundet bin
oder war, (leider sind inzwischen viele von ihnen verstorben), mehr oder
weniger frei kopiert und in dieses Bild integriert.

Alle anderen Personen, Bildlegenden, Geschichten und »Weisheiten«
sind erfunden.

<u>Glossary</u>

The tragic life of the "Elephant Man" Joseph Carey Merrick
(1862 to 1890) was filmed in 1980 by David Lynch based on true
events with a star cast.

The quotes by Sigmund Freud and Albert Einstein are original quotes.

The vaudeville artist "Monsieur Antoine" never existed, but his alleged
twin brother, the flatulence artist Josef Puiol (1857 to 1945), who
celebrated international success with his "art" (flatulence artist is a
so-called art farter).

Both the New York Times and American Medicine published in 1907 a
report, according to which the American physician Duncan MacDougall
(1866 to 1920) allegedly could prove after many experiments that the
human soul weighs on average of 21g. However, it is not proven that he
determined the weight of the soul of a hippopotamus.

In the picture "Alois Gürtelbaum, red wine drinker and art collector" I
have more or less freely copied pictures of artists with whom I am or
was friends for years, (unfortunately many of them are now deceased)
and integrated them into this picture.

All other characters, captions, stories and "wisdom" are fictitious.

Jonas C. Haefeli

1947	geboren und aufgewachsen in Zürich in einem kulturell geprägten Elternhaus Erste Begegnung mit Film und Theater als Kinderdarsteller beim Schweizer Fernsehen und in Kino-Werbefilmen
1964	Auftritte vorwiegend mit Jazz-, aber auch mit Pop-Formationen, zuerst als Schlagzeuger, später auch als Flötist/Saxofonist
1965	Mitbegründer und Co-Leiter des Kultur-Clubs »Platte 27« Bühnenbild-Assistenz am Schauspielhaus Zürich intensive Konzerttätigkeit in verschiedenen Clubs und Festivals im In- und Ausland
1966	Eröffnung und Leitung der »Galerie Platte 27« in Zürich Nebenjobs als Tontechniker und Aufnahme-/ Produktionsleiter bei Filmproduktionen
1969	Regieassistenz beim ersten Deutschen Fernsehen
1970	Erster größerer Kompositions-Auftrag von der ARD Nachfolgend vorwiegend als Film- und Theaterkomponist tätig Vertonung von ca. 50 TV- und Kino-Spielfilmen: Die Schweizermacher, Der Erfinder, Klassezämekunft, Hannibal, Mann ohne Gedächtnis, Der Stumme, u.a. mehrere Folgen der Serien Tatort, Schwarz-Rot-Gold, Der Eugen, Diverse Dokumentar- und TV-/Kino Werbefilme Bühnenmusik für das Schauspielhaus Zürich, u.a. Hörspiele für Radio SRF und Features für Fernsehen SRF Mehrere CD-Produktionen

Dazwischen Tontechniker bei Dokumentarfilmproduktionen in Afghanistan, Iran, Tansania, Portugal, sowie eine abenteuerliche Überquerung des Pazifik mit einem kleinen, alten Segelschiff, anschließend mehrmonatiger Aufenthalt auf den Marquesas-Inseln in der Südsee

2007 Herausgabe des Bildbandes »Poesie des Unmöglichen«

Lebt mit der Schauspielerin Elisabeth Berger in Zürich
und in Uetikon am See

1947	born and grown up in Zurich in a culturally home with a strong cultural influence First encounter with film and theater as a child actor on Swiss television and in cinema commercials
1964	Performances mainly with jazz but also with pop formations, first as drummer, later also as flutist/saxophonist
1965	Co-founder and co-leader of the cultural club "Platte 27" Stage design assistant at the Schauspielhaus Zurich, intensive concert activity in various clubs and festivals at home and abroad
1966	opening and management of the "Galerie Platte 27" in Zurich, side jobs as sound engineer and recording/production manager for film productions
1969	Assistant director at the First German Television
1970	First major composition commission from the ARD (German TV), subsequently mainly active as a film and theater composer scoring of approx. 50 TV and cinema feature films: Die Schweizermacher, Der Erfinder, Klassezämekunft, Hannibal, Mann ohne Gedächtnis, Der Stumme, and others several episodes of the series Tatort, Schwarz-Rot-Gold, Der Eugen, Various documentaries and TV/cinema commercials Stage music for the Schauspielhaus Zurich, among others Radio plays for Radio SRF and features for Television SRF, Several CD productions

In between sound engineer for documentary film productions in Afghanistan, Iran, Tanzania, Portugal, as well as venturous crossing of the Pacific Ocean with a small, old sailing ship, followed by a stay of several months on the Marquesas Islands in the South Seas

2007 Publication of the picture book "Poetry of the Impossible"

Lives with the actress Elisabeth Berger in Zurich
and in Uetikon am See